D0175324

# SHAKE
# OFF
# THE
# DUST

# JAY STRACK

# SHAKE
# OFF
# THE
# DUST

*Leaving Your Past Behind and Getting On with the Rest of Your Life*

THOMAS NELSON PUBLISHERS

*Nashville*

Published in Nashville, Tennessee, by Thomas Nelson, Inc., and distributed in Canada by Lawson Falle, Ltd., Cambridge, Ontario.

Printed in the United States of America.

Scripture quotations are from THE NEW KING JAMES VERSION of the Bible. Copyright © 1979, 1980, 1982, Thomas Nelson, Inc., Publishers.

**LIBRARY OF CONGRESS**
**Library of Congress Cataloging-in-Publication Data**

Strack, Jay.
　Shake off the dust / Jay Strack.
　　p.　　cm.
　Bibliography: p.
　ISBN 0-8407-7624-1
　1. Christian life—1960–　2. Church and social problems.
3. Strack, Jay.　I. Title.
BV4501.2.S796　1988
248.4—dc19　　　　　　　　　　　　　　88–5372
　　　　　　　　　　　　　　　　　　　　CIP

*To* H. Fred Williams,
*preacher, educator, man of God,*
*my father in the ministry;*
*to all those who, by their example*
*and unconditional love,*
*helped a troubled young man*
*to shake off the dust;*
*and*
*to my wife, Diane,*
*whose unconditional love*
*has helped*
*me more than anyone*
*on this planet*
*to shake off the dust*
*and enjoy my life in Christ.*

# CONTENTS

HOPE FOR THE FUTURE

# PREFACE

GROWING UP HAS always been difficult. But for some kids it's a nightmare. I was one of those kids. Growing up in a broken home in Florida in the 1960s was tough, but being a teenager in the 1970s was even worse!

Every time I turned around somebody was trying to get me to drink this or swallow that. "Just grab a handful, man. Any color'll do," a friend once said, as he offered me a handful of pills in various colors, shapes, and sizes.

"I'm not into that," I replied.

"Hey, what harm can it do?" he challenged. Because I couldn't instantly come up with a good answer, I gave in and grabbed a handful. It wasn't long until I succumbed to the danger of the mysterious pills and, unfortunately, learned the answer the hard way.

Mine is a tough story. My childhood was marred with physical and emotional abuse. My teenage years were marked by drug and alcohol abuse. I began taking drugs at thirteen and was a serious user by fifteen. By sixteen I had been busted for selling drugs and had to face the fact that I was a teenage junkie.

Most of the people I meet are struggling to shake off the dust from their lives and don't seem able to escape their problems. Some can't even talk about them. Others are willing to talk, but seem incapable of doing anything about the problems.

There is a story in the Bible about a woman who was hunchbacked all of her life (Luke 13:10–13). She spent a lifetime looking down at the dirt until Jesus straightened her out. Most people are like that woman. They can only see themselves and their problems. They don't look up and see how close their salvation really is.

As a teenage junkie I finally looked up and saw Jesus Christ. I want to help you see that there is hope for a better life. You don't have to remain victimized by your past. Whatever has gone wrong can be made right. Some problems involve the scars of memory. They are the results of things done to us by others. And some are the consequences of things we have done to ourselves. Each problem is unique to itself. But all can be solved in Christ.

Many others have been delivered from the mistakes of the past, and they have given me permission to tell their stories in order to share the hope of new life to you who may be bound by the chains of the past.

Each has a powerful story to tell. Their experiences will both shock you and grip your heart with compassion. I have changed their names to protect their identity and privacy, but who they are is not nearly so important as what they have experienced.

Our society has been in upheaval since before the 1960s. Things have changed drastically in the past thirty years. The society that once was, is no more. Today's family is torn by divorce, abuse, alcohol, and drugs. The very fabric of American society is coming apart at the seams. It won't be long until we have torn it apart completely—unless something is done about it now.

I am constantly confronted with people seeking hope. That is what my ministry is all about—hope for a better life. No matter what has gone wrong in your life, you can find a better way. You don't have to carry around the dirt of your past mistakes. Get up, shake off the dust, and go on.

# SHAKE
# OFF
# THE
# DUST

# SCARS OF THE PAST

# Chapter 1 ◀

# Will You Be My Daddy?

THE WARM FLORIDA rain beat hard against the pavement as I peered out the window, waiting for my father to come home. My nose pressed against the glass, I stared ahead blankly.

"Don't worry, honey. Daddy will be here soon," Mom called from the kitchen of our suburban home.

I used to stand at the window and watch for hours, faithfully waiting for my father to come home from work. At the same time, I always wondered what he'd be like when he came in. I could remember all the times he had come home drunk, looking for a fight. When he got like that, anything could set him off. This was to be one of those days.

Time plodded on endlessly. The rain finally stopped and the muggy, humid haze of central Florida fell over the neighborhood like a thick blanket.

Finally, at dusk, a car pulled into the driveway. Dad was home! Beaming with hope, I watched Dad slowly step out of the car. But when he began to stagger up the rain-soaked driveway toward the house, my hope turned to fear.

The door burst open and the arguing began. "Where have you been all this time?" I heard Mom demand.

"None of your business," he snapped back.

Soon they were at it full blast. I ran to the doorway, clasping my hands tightly against my ears. Mom spotted me out of the corner of her eye.

"Go to your room!" she ordered. "You don't need to listen to this!" But I retreated only partway down the hall.

"I've had all I can take," Mom screamed.

"So have I!" Dad returned. "I'm leaving for good this time! There's no good reason to stay."

*He can't mean it,* I insisted to myself. *I must be the reason. He won't just leave us here. Surely he won't leave me too.*

But Dad began to pack his belongings and load them into the car. Torn by disbelief, Mom watched helplessly, tears streaming down her face. She couldn't believe her husband was actually leaving for good.

"Aren't you going to change your mind?" she finally asked.

"No," he replied firmly. "This is it!" He turned and walked out the door for the final time. Unable to stand still any longer, I burst out of the house and grabbed him by the legs.

"Daddy, please don't go," I sobbed. "Please don't leave us!" He tried to be kind and held me for a moment, but finally pushed me away and drove off. My heart was broken. Tears poured down my face as I stood there feeling confused and rejected. *He will come back,* I thought. *He has to.*

"Come on in," Mom called after me. "There's nothing else we can do now."

That night seemed like an eternity of hopeless anxiety as I drifted in and out of sleep. *Maybe if I'd been better, Daddy wouldn't have left us,* I thought. I tossed and turned, trying to figure out how to get him back.

As the days passed, though, it became increasingly obvious that Daddy wasn't coming back. The money soon ran out; and Mom, my younger brother, and I began a series of moves to smaller houses in lower income neighborhoods. Mom had to work two jobs to make ends meet, so she had little time at home. In desperation she finally gave my younger brother to her parents to raise. For all practical purposes I had lost everyone—father, brother, even my mother. Loneliness overwhelmed me.

Mom hurt for everyone. But as much as she wished circumstances could be different, she felt helpless to change them. Dad eventually lost everything because of his excessive drinking, and Mom became bitter, blaming Dad for everything that had gone wrong in our lives. When the financial pressure and fatigue got the best of her, she threatened to send me to Dad, whom she portrayed as a wicked and cruel man. Again, I was caught by the fear of rejection, but this time, by my mother.

When I was nine years old, Mom married a commercial fisherman named Bob. Life seemed as if it would get better for a while. Bob told me to call him Dad. We bought a small house in a better area and even had a color TV and a new car. *Finally,* I thought, *we are a real family.*

But like my first dad, Bob had a serious drinking problem, and he and Mom argued constantly. In the little stucco block houses of our neighborhood, you could hear everybody's business up and down the block. Mom's and Bob's arguments often got out of hand, and several times the neighbors called the police to break up their fights.

The first time the police cars came with lights flashing and sirens blaring, half the neighborhood showed up out of curiosity. I was so embarrassed I was afraid to go out and face the neighborhood kids the next day. Yet despite all this, I was excited about having a new dad. I felt normal and accepted.

Then one day, my world was shattered again. Mom told me her marriage was over and Bob was leaving. "He's at the Surf Club," Mom announced. "I'm going down there, but if he doesn't come home, it's over."

I jumped in the car with her, hopeful that Bob would return. I wanted a dad under any conditions: I needed Bob.

Panic seized me as we rode along. Tears welling up in my eyes, I prayed silently, "God, please don't let me lose this daddy."

While Mom went into the bar, I sat in the car, crying, hoping, and praying that she would be able to persuade Bob to come home. But in a few minutes she returned alone. Slumping into the seat, she rested her head against the steering wheel for a moment. Then she looked up with determined anger and said, "Let's go; he's not coming."

I bolted out of the car and burst into the club. Peering through the smoke-filled darkness, I spotted him sitting at the bar. I ran up to him and pleaded desperately that he come home. Bob tried to turn away, but I kept crying, "You promised to be my dad! Please, don't go. Please!"

Finally, he grasped my shoulders, looked me in the eyes, and said, "If you get down and beg, I'll come home with you." Innocently and sincerely, I got down on my knees and began to beg. But to my amazement, Bob burst out laughing. With a quick shove, he ordered me to get lost.

That moment something snapped inside. I wasn't sure what was happening at the time, but I couldn't cope with any more rejection, so I hardened to protect myself. I vowed that night to never again care for anyone or ask anyone to care for me. *From now on,* I thought, *I'll take care of myself. I don't need anybody.*

The carefree innocence of childhood ended for me. A light turned off in my soul, and a line was drawn across the path of my life. Things would never be the same.

In the years that followed, my life went from bad to worse. Mother constantly reached out for happiness, but never found it. Men came and went from our lives regularly, but I ignored them all, determined not to get hurt again. In the meantime, my real father sank further and further into alcoholism, unable to hold a steady job. He, too, was searching for answers but came up empty-handed.

The unstable circumstances made me feel like a termite in a yo-yo. But one thing never changed. I never let myself care about the men who came into my life. I kept everyone at a distance, including my mother.

One of my stepfathers had a teenage son by another marriage. When the two moved in, the teenager molested me and threatened to kill me if I ever told anyone. Bitter and confused, I withdrew even further into myself, afraid to tell anyone for fear

I would be rejected again. I can see now that my distrust of everyone grew from my feeling that everyone had hurt me in one way or another. And though I withdrew, I desperately wanted to be loved. I wanted to reach out but saw no one there to reach back.

Through all of my troubles, I developed an intense hatred for alcohol. It had ruined my life: it had taken my father, sent away my brother, and demoralized my mother. "If there is one thing I'll never do," I vowed, "it is take a drink."

As a teenager, I was insecure and overweight—mad at the world and mad at myself. I used to shuffle along with a "loser's limp" that revealed my lack of confidence. I was often alone. The house was empty when I got home from school each afternoon. I felt that life had let me down. Any happy memories I had had as a child now blurred in my mind, and the present seemed an endless parade of disappointment.

With all my negative thinking, I easily fell prey to teenage peer pressure. My interest in slot cars and movies gave way to following the crowd, chewing tobacco, and smoking dope. I wanted to be accepted so badly I would do anything to get attention, but I usually drove away more people than I attracted. Although I became the class clown, my mouthy, smart-aleck personality was only a cover-up for my inner turmoil.

My big break came in junior high when I made the football team. *Now I can make it,* I thought. *I'm finally one of the cool kids.*

After a game one night the captain of the team brought out a case of beer and began to pass it around. I was shocked. "Don't you realize what this stuff can do to you?" I asked.

"Yeah, isn't it great!" someone replied.

"But you guys don't realize what this stuff has done to my dad and to our family!"

"Come on, kid. You're not afraid, are you?" the team captain challenged.

"Chicken!" somebody shouted. "Maybe you ought to go home." But that was the *last* place I wanted to be.

Suddenly, I found myself doing what I had vowed I would never do—drinking alcohol. It tasted awful, but everyone acted like they were having such a great time that I went along with them.

I began to drink in excess regularly, and the very actions and attitudes I had despised in others became evident in my own life. I wanted to drink away my problems. I went to endless parties where almost everyone got drunk and where, some nights, I got very sick. But I kept insisting I was having a great time.

For me, as for so many others, alcohol was a "gateway" drug that led to other drug addictions. I was unaware of the cycle that alcohol would lead me into. But it wasn't long before I began to smoke marijuana, which led to my taking pills and then hallucinogenics. Finally, I shot speed. I began to sink further and further into drug abuse. Mom loved me but didn't know how to express her love, nor did she know how to control or discipline me.

I didn't see that I was caught in the middle of the revolutionary social upheaval of the late 1960s and 1970s, and I couldn't cope. Although outwardly I appeared to be a rebel with a raised fist, inwardly I was empty and confused. My world changed. It revolved around my friends, not my family. I stayed on the streets to avoid going home to an empty house. I failed most of my classes and was kicked off the football team. My excessive drug use led to a sense of apathy about life; I just didn't seem to care anymore.

Like many teenagers whose lives are dominated by drugs, I began to wonder if life was really worth living at all. I couldn't seem to get my life together. Thoughts of suicide occasionally flashed through my mind, and I began to display self-destructive tendencies. I drove at reckless speeds, took foolish risks, and accepted dares, like that of jumping off a causeway into the gulf. I wondered what was wrong with me, but I seemed helpless to do anything about it.

Eventually, I was arrested four times for drug possession with the intent to distribute and driving under the influence, and sent to the Lee County Detention Center in Ft. Myers. The first three arrests were considered minor, and I spent only one night in the detention center each time. But the last arrest was much more serious.

I lost control of my car one night while hallucinating from drugs and hit a whole row of taxicabs, causing thousands of dollars worth of damage. Panicked, I jumped out of the car and ran away. The police pursued and apprehended me for hit-and-run, possession, and being under the influence of drugs. To make things worse, I punched the arresting officer. By the time the judge was through with me, I had lost my license and been sentenced to three months in the detention center.

In the detention center I was alone with myself and my thoughts. The friends I had lived for forgot all about me. There were no girls, no parties, no rock 'n' roll, and not even a television. A few kids wrote me, and one even soaked LSD on the back of the stamp so I could lick it. But that was little consolation for the isolation I endured. I was out of control. Sometimes I cried myself to sleep, and other times I tossed and turned on my bed, agonizing over all that had gone wrong.

Through it all, Mom tried to stand by me. She was confused and embarrassed, but she hurt for me. Somehow, she felt partly to blame, but she didn't know how to help me. "If I had just been a better mother," she'd say. We would try to talk about all we had been through, but each time the conversations ended in blank silence.

Every time I was busted for drugs, I would vow I'd quit. I would endure the withdrawals at the detention center—perspiration engulfing my body, endless diarrhea. Through shakes and nausea, I would wonder, *Why can't I give it up?* And I would quit. I quit a hundred times. But I went right back.

I did, however, become increasingly aware that drugs were a dead-end street. Many of my heroes on the rock music scene had died from drug overdoses. I identified with the words one of the singers on the dead-end drug habit had written shortly before his death: "There must be some way out of here."

The doctors at the detention center told me I was getting

to be a lost cause. They said I had to want help, but nobody seemed to understand. I *did* want help, but I didn't know where to turn.

I spent my seventeenth birthday scrubbing floors in the detention center. *Nobody really cares,* I thought. *I'm all alone and nobody cares.* I felt as if time had run out for me, as if I were an old man whose body was used up. My mind was blurry; I had lost all hope. And there in my cell, I came to the end of myself.

I have chosen to share my story with you in the hope that it will help you to understand and handle the same kinds of hurts that I have felt. It is written from my heart in the belief that there truly is a better way to live.

At my most desperate hour, I found the way of escape from the chemical prison to which I had sentenced myself. I found out what really makes life worth living. And above all, I found out how to *shake off the dust* of my past. I learned that I didn't have to carry the dirt and guilt of my past any longer. What happened to me can happen to you also.

# Chapter 2 ◄

# A Real
# Father
# This Time

THE SUMMER OF 1970 stretched on as though it would
never end. Being held in detention for three months was not
exactly my idea of the ideal way to spend a Florida summer. I
was angry and confused. But one thing was clear—I had to do
whatever was necessary to get out of that place!

"You can go back to school in the fall, Jay," announced the
detention officer. "That is," he added, "if you are on good behavior."

I remember sitting on the edge of my bed in the stark,
dormitory-like room wondering if fall would ever come. *How
could I let myself get into this kind of mess?* I thought. Day
after day, I reviewed my young life, telling myself, *This isn't
happiness. Life has to be better than this.* During those hot
summer months I promised myself I would quit drugs for good.

Drug addiction is an endless cycle of imprisonment. You
get high in order to forget your problems; but getting high creates new problems, and you have to get high again to avoid
those problems. In time the highs are more difficult to attain; in
fact, each high is lower than the last one. The addict then begins to sink lower and lower into hopeless futility.

Instead of getting higher, the addict becomes lonelier,
more helpless, desperate, and confused; no wonder so many die
from drug addiction. The pull of suicide is incredible. Once a

person loses self-control, he loses all resistance to chemical dependency. He gives in to the drug even when he knows it's going to harm him. Because dizziness, nausea, and vomiting are part of the drug user's experience, most kids don't want to be alone while they take drugs. Instead, they try to talk someone else into doing it too.

For me, drugs provided an escape from my problems and failures. I perceived fantasy as reality; I felt at peace with myself and all my troubles disappeared while I was high. Drugs gave me a false sense of power and control. But when the high ended, I crashed back down to reality in brutal despair. That was what made my life so tough. I couldn't stay up all the time. So each crash created the need to get high all over again. Trapped in this vicious cycle, I lost all sense of hope and responsibility. I felt like a helpless victim.

I began drinking on weekends and soon progressed to drinking every day. Alcohol was always available. Some kids brought it from home. Others bought it illegally from store owners who wanted to make a buck, even from minors. The availability of alcohol was one of my greatest pressures. It always seemed to be there at the parties, the football games, the races, the rock concerts or wherever I went.

I smoked my first joint on a dare. I didn't want to be different or excluded from the rest of the group, so I gave in to their pressure. Soon I was smoking it regularly. The harsh smoke began to taste sweeter. I liked what it did to me. It gave me a quicker and more pleasant high than alcohol ever had.

I soon learned that once you cross the line to marijuana, it becomes easier to say yes to any kind of drugs. I began taking anything people offered me. I liked amphetamines ("speed") the best because they created an instant rush and left me high for hours.

As I sat in the detention center, I was lower than I had ever been. Life had hit the bottom and drugs had taken me there. *I've got to quit,* I kept telling myself. *All of this will be different when I get out of here,* I promised myself. But it wasn't.

The day I was finally released from the Lee County Detention Center, I was ready to make a new start, but I felt too weak to do it. I was afraid to fail. I didn't want to let down my parents or my brother. I was in a civil war with myself. My moods swung drastically from bitterness to depression to anger. I would call out to God for help and then turn right around and shake my fist at Him in anger. I had seen enough of the detention center to know I didn't want to go back to it ever again. But I didn't know how to quit.

When school started up in the fall, it didn't take long for me to fall right back into the routine of getting high every day. Kids were passing around drugs like first graders trading candy at lunch. Drugs were everywhere. Guys were selling dope in the bathrooms, the hallways, the cafeteria, and sometimes even in class! But the most prominent place to get drugs at our school was "The Bridge," a wooden bridge behind the football field connecting the parking lot for lower classmen with the senior parking lot. It was the spot where fights took place, where couples made out, and where kids smoked and bought drugs.

I never had a big-time drug pusher try to sell me drugs. I got it from my friends. If my friends hadn't been dealers, I possibly could have stayed clean a little longer. But they were, and I didn't.

I was angry and frustrated. I was mad at myself, mad at drugs, and mad at the world. I didn't fit anywhere. I certainly didn't agree with the adult mentality known then as the establishment. I felt that they were only against drugs because they didn't understand them. The truth is they were all using nicotine, alcohol and prescription drugs regularly. To me they were all a bunch of hypocrites.

But I was no longer comfortable with casual drug users either. They were so naive! They thought this was all a silly game. But I knew it wasn't. I knew it was a very dangerous and deadly game.

But I didn't want to be one of the serious drug users and the junkies either. I couldn't see myself as hooked as they were. But I was fast becoming just like them. After all I had been through, I still couldn't quit. I was enjoying it less, but doing it more. I felt trapped and I was trapped. Realizing that I had no way out of my addiction pulled me down even further. "It's a lost cause," I thought. "I'm not going to make it."

By November, I was desperate for help. On the outside I covered up like everyone else. But inside, I was hurting. "God, please help me," I prayed. But I did not know how to find God. I was empty and my life was more meaningless than ever.

I figured a lot of my mess was God's fault. Why hadn't He made my dad stay? Where was He when I was abused and rejected? Why had He let my friends die? Did He even love me? It didn't seem possible after all I'd done. I felt dirty and guilty in addition to the loneliness. I wanted to blame God, but I also wanted His help.

During this time Charlie, a guy at school, invited me to a Bible study. Charlie stood out from the rest of the gang. He was clean-cut and usually smiling, and everyone knew he didn't use drugs. He consistently invited me to Bible study and daily told me about a God of love who wanted to be my heavenly Father. I'd had enough bad experiences with fathers in my life, so I kept declining. But Charlie really seemed to care about what happened to me, even when I was unkind to him.

On Thanksgiving weekend I went with some friends to a rock concert in Miami. We took along our usual supply of alcohol and drugs for a real party night. But that night the high didn't satisfy; it just wasn't enough. For the first time I admitted the emptiness in my life. I saw the immorality and hopelessness around me, and I began to feel guilty about my sin.

Charlie's standing invitation to the Bible study suddenly appealed to me. He had told me over and over, "I care. I'm praying for you." That night I believed him, and the next night I found myself turning my car onto Central Avenue and driving to a small green stucco house where the Bible study was held. Pulling into the driveway, I realized that I had probably driven by this house most of my life. I had driven down Central Avenue to go to the mall, to school, and to many of my friends' homes.

The house looked harmless enough, but still, I was nervous. I almost turned the car around and left, but the hope of peace and happiness without drugs made me stay. I had heard a little about this place from some kids at school. They told me about the young leader, Rick, who could talk about the Bible in a language even I could understand. I decided to go in.

Charlie had said to "come as you are," so I showed up in cut-off jeans and sandals. As soon as the door opened, I felt a flood of warmth and love. No one stared at my hair or my clothes. Instead, I was greeted by hugs and acceptance. An older woman, who I learned later was Rick's mother, smiled and said, "Welcome, son."

The small room was crowded. I recognized several kids from school, which made me immediately put up a front. "I'm just here to get Charlie off my back," I joked. But they seemed genuinely glad to see me, so after a little while I relaxed. Someone handed me a Bible, and sitting cross-legged on the floor, I listened as kids all around me talked about how real Jesus was in their lives. They were excited about knowing Him personally and getting strength from the Bible. I was curious but skeptical.

The more I listened, however, the more I began to sense the reality of God in their lives. My world of drugs now seemed a nightmarish fantasy. Could this new life have real meaning? Could I really know God? Who was I kidding? My life was a mess! But this God seemed to be my only hope.

Then it was Rick's turn to speak. All eyes were riveted on him. He opened his Bible and read from 2 Timothy, chapter 3. I didn't know much about the Bible—in fact, I had never read one in my life—but I found myself listening intently. Rick described a life without God as one full of self-love, empty boasting, pride, rebellion, immorality, and unnatural affections. What could be more unnatural, I wondered, *than loving to inhale smoke, drink poison, or stick a needle in my arm?* Little did I realize that the Bible would mirror my life as it really was.

Rick went on to explain that our actions are symptoms of our problem, rather than the problem itself. "The real problem," he explained, "is the emptiness within man, which only God can truly fill." I realized then that I had been trying to fill my empty life with everything but God. I already felt guilty. I knew I was a sinner. But Rick added that God loved us just the way we were—with all our bitterness, anger, sin, and rebellion.

I wore a surfer cross, which was popular then, and had seen crosses everywhere; but for the first time, I understood what the cross was all about. The same One whose name I'd taken in vain loved me enough to die for me on that cross. The most life-changing aspect of what I heard was that Jesus had risen again and that He is alive today.

I had briefly experimented with Zen Buddhism, but from Rick I heard about a God who had power over life and death. Could He give me power to live without drugs? Could He fill the emptiness in my life? I had to find out.

As Rick brought the evening's message to a close, he stressed that every individual must make a personal choice to accept Christ as Savior. He told us that a simple prayer of belief, asking for forgiveness, was all that would be necessary to receive a new life and a new heart. This was God's promise to us. "Call upon the Lord," he said, "and He will answer you."

Promises! So many had broken their promises to me and I'd broken so many myself. Could I trust this God of love and forgiveness when I felt so unlovable and couldn't forgive myself? I had to learn to trust and to ask for help. It was something I had said I would never do again.

Rick pressed the issue further and asked those of us who had never done so to accept this Savior. "The *something* you're looking for is a *Someone*," he said. A peace fell over me that I had never before experienced. Confusion gave way to understanding. Rebellion gave way to God's love filling my heart. *But what if I can't live up to this?* I thought. *I've tried to change before and have failed.* Almost as if he were reading my mind, Rick said, "You don't have to change first. Just come as you are. God will put His Holy Spirit inside of you and give you His power. He'll do the changing as you trust Him." He asked all those who wanted this new life to raise their hands.

I decided to trust Someone again. I raised my hand and prayed with him to receive this new life. After several hours at the Bible study, I went home with a joy I'd never known. I had a peace that my past was forgiven—a new power to help with today and hope for tomorrow. I knew I would no longer be alone in my struggle. For the first time in my life I felt like I had a Father who wouldn't leave me. This time, I had a real dad! He was a spiritual Father who would meet all the needs in my life. But I still had to face all my old friends and all the old temptations at school.

The very next week a guy gave me one-hundred-dollars worth of good speed. "Just take it," he said, shoving it into my hands.

"But I don't want it," I tried to say, as he hurried off. As I stood there holding the package I wondered what I was supposed to do. *I can't just throw this away.* But God seemed to speak directly to me. "Oh yes you can! Get rid of that stuff, Jay," He seemed to say.

I hesitated only a moment before I walked to the boys' room and flushed it all down the toilet. You cannot imagine the joy and relief I felt! I had said no to drugs and I felt great about it! I was free and the past no longer had a hold on me.

The first weeks of my new life were filled with joy and excitement. My euphoria about being free from drugs was greater than any high I had ever experienced on drugs. A few months later, though, like every alcoholic or drug addict, I "hit the wall." The initial withdrawals had been tough, but this was the toughest time in my life. I had felt so free, but now I was depressed and didn't know why. It seemed like the ghost of my past kept haunting me: "Who do you think you are? You're just a junkie and you know it."

I began to experience a series of flashbacks to the problems that had driven me to drugs in the first place. Although I had come to know God personally, I still had to face the consequences of my earlier behavior. I still had to go to court; I had poor grades from years of not studying; I distrusted people. I wanted to run away from it all.

I decided to get alone, so I went to Ft. Myers Beach and sat on the sand. As I struggled with the aftershock of depression, I began to write all of my sins in the sand. The list got longer and longer. But as the tide kept coming in, the waves began to wash away the list. As I sat there watching, I realized that God's grace had washed away my sins. I watched until the water covered the list and it was completely gone.

*That is what God has done for me,* I thought. *He has washed away my sins. I don't need to let the past get me down anymore. It's gone forever.* When I stood up to leave, the sun was setting in splendid hues of red and gold against the clouds on the horizon of the Gulf. The warm air felt fresh and clean, and so did I.

God worked in my life as my senior year proceeded. I didn't understand a lot of things, but I took a strong and aggressive stand for Christ at school. Kids called me Moses because I wore long hair and sandals, carried my Bible to school, and witnessed regularly. Several kids teased me about my "religion." Others were skeptical about what I had done. Some even took bets that it wouldn't last. I began to learn who my real friends were. The old gang had no use for me anymore. I was different and they wanted no part of it.

I didn't always have a lot of tact, but I did have a God-given sense of boldness. I quickly learned that God develops us to our full potential. He changes us, but He also uses and perfects our natural abilities. My sarcasm turned into a natural sense of humor, and my antagonism turned into a positive boldness to witness to others.

"Jay, you're crazy," old friends would say. "You've given up everything fun in life."

"No I haven't," I replied. "I'm having more fun than I've ever had!"

As I got my eyes off myself and focused on the needs of others, I began to realize that many had problems worse than my own. I began reaching out to help them. I became part of the solution instead of part of the problem. It felt great to be on the other side. I soon developed a desire to invest my life in helping others. I wanted to reach out to everyone I could and help them find the answers to their problems.

Throughout that year I continued to attend the Bible studies at the Milams' house on Central Avenue. My hunger for the Bible grew intensely, but like most of the Jesus Movement converts, I lacked guidance and maturity. We had little adult leadership and virtually no contact with any local church; in fact, we weren't even welcome in most churches. But we were convinced they were all boring and hypocritical anyway.

We were so excited about the things of God, we would stay up half the night talking about the Bible. We studied it, debated it, and continually exhorted one another. In a sense, the group became our family.

Most of the new cults that sprang up at that time were called the "family," and the leader was looked upon as the "dad." I am convinced that kids were looking for substitutes for their parents who they felt had let them down. While our group was certainly not a cult in a theological sense, it did function like one.

We were an entity unto ourselves, isolated from the rest of the body of Christ. We were independent and self-sufficient. No one told us what to believe. We found out for ourselves what the Bible had to say.

I eventually came to see the dangers in such groups. Theological error, self-opinion, and misunderstanding easily predominated, and some of those Bible study groups even went into cultic heresy. But there were positive elements about the Jesus Movement that the traditional churches needed. We had an intense love for Christ and for one another that some churches never experienced. We had an excitement about the Bible and a boldness in witnessing that most Christians missed.

The Jesus Movement had a family atmosphere. Everyone felt welcome. They were accepted as a part of the group. There was no hypocrisy or social game playing. People felt free to express themselves openly about anything without fear of rejection. In many ways, we felt that we had found the atmosphere of the ideal New Testament church. We were filled with wonder, worship, excitement, and expectation for the future.

As I began to grow in my newfound faith, I came to realize that God was filling the void in my life. His love and acceptance replaced my need for acceptance by my peers. His joy and power became greater than anything I had ever experienced on drugs. My life was filled with hope. I had a new direction and a new sense of purpose.

## Chapter 3

# Lord,
# I'll Go
# Anywhere

I WAS GRADUATED from high school in 1971, unsure of what would come next in my life. I had barely made it out of high school, so my going to college seemed like an impossible dream. My life had been changed, but now the Bible study group was breaking up. Many of the kids were joining various local churches. Some were going away to college, and still others were simply dropping out. I decided to take a part-time job as a traveling salesman. It was lonely, but it was a living.

November brought my first birthday as a Christian, and I was beginning to feel unsure about how to live in the Christian life. My only real spiritual experience had been in the Bible study group; but the membership had dwindled to a handful, and I hadn't attended in a while. I had been warned of "hitting the wall," an expression used by drug addicts to describe the first big temptation to fall after months of feeling great. A sudden depression and emptiness set in for which I had no explanation.

At graduation many of my classmates had scoffed at my beliefs saying, "You'll get over it. We'll party again in the fall." Their words now ran through my mind, and I began to wonder if it was worth it all. I prayed for direction and knew I needed the encouragement of Christian friends. I also needed someone to date. *But where would I find a girl who believed like me?* I thought.

By December, I decided to drop in again on the Bible study at Milam's. I was immediately disappointed by the size of the group. But I met an unusual girl named Diane Raso. She was my age and also a dedicated Christian. When we were introduced, Diane bubbled over with enthusiasm as she described to me her love of evangelism. I could hardly believe what I was hearing. Here was a girl who shared many of my hopes and dreams. *Could she be the one for me?* I asked myself. *Is she the friend for whom I've prayed so long?*

Diane encouraged me to go to her church with her and I eventually agreed. In time, I got up the nerve to ask her for a date. I was so excited when she said yes that I bought new clothes, cleaned up my car, and planned for the big night out. Diane, however, had other ideas.

When I arrived, she was dressed casually and suggested we stay home and study the Bible. If that wasn't enough, her mother and younger sister joined us for hot chocolate and cookies! I felt like we were re-enacting a scene from a *Leave It to Beaver* episode. I left angry and frustrated. *She is history,* I thought. *I'd die if anyone knew we stayed home with her mother.*

In the meantime, I struggled with my own life. I tried to stay straight, but I had little or no encouragement from home, school, or friends. Whenever I was with my old friends from high school, I was uncomfortable. I felt like I didn't belong anywhere. I slipped into being a lukewarm Christian—unhappy with my spiritual life, but uncomfortable with the world.

New Year's Eve approached and I almost succumbed to the old gang's invitation to party. Then I remembered the emptiness of my old life.

"No, I can't go back to that," I thought. "It's a dead-end street."

Instead, I called Diane. She was glad to hear from me and we decided to get together on New Year's Eve.

I wondered if her mom would be there. But then it hit me. I had prayed for a straight girl, a strong Christian who could help me mature as a Christian. God had answered my prayer with Diane and I hadn't even realized it.

At midnight we got down on our knees together and re-dedicated ourselves to live for God and tell others about Him. As we prayed, I felt a bond with Diane. She was the right kind of girl for me and I knew it.

We began attending a Bible study led by friends of Diane's family. The parents had opened their home to kids who wanted to know Christ and grow spiritually, and the study was led by their son, Anthony. Although I was still very uncomfortable with traditional churches and resisted attending as often as I could, Anthony spent hours with me, helping me grow, answering my questions, and giving me the support and care I needed. In many ways he became my new pastor, taking up where Rick had left off.

By Easter, Diane and I were deeply in love. I wanted to get married, establish a Christian home, and raise a family. I hoped to erase the bad memories of my childhood with a new life. Easter morning I surprised Diane with a stuffed bunny wearing a promise ring. It was all I could afford, but it was enough to thrill Diane and me. After all, we were both only eighteen.

We were so excited we couldn't wait to tell Diane's parents. What a shock it was to find out they were totally against our marrying. I had barely made it out of high school. I didn't have a full-time job. I was from a broken home. Their list of objections seemed endless. They threatened to break up our relationship. Even my mother begged me not to get married. So I decided to prove them all wrong and hit the road as a salesman. I was on my way to the top. Everyone thought that once we got away from each other, the infatuation would wear off, but we knew better.

The life of a traveling salesman was a lonely life. I hated it. I had no Bible study group, no friends, and no church. But this time I had someone praying for me, writing to me, and sharing all my hopes and dreams. Diane really loved me and would not give up on us. During those lonely days, I grew to love her more and more.

My sales job gave me many opportunities to share my faith. I witnessed to everyone I met and told them about Jesus Christ and the hope and forgiveness He promises to all who trust in Him. I was excited about Christ and what He was doing in my life. But it bothered me that I didn't have anywhere to send those I led to Christ for Christian growth and fellowship.

One evening I heard a dynamic, humorous, and flamboyant evangelist named Bob Harrington, known as the Chaplain of Bourbon Street. Unlike any preacher I had ever heard, he laughed and joked, yet he preached with power and conviction.

I wanted to talk to him in person, just to tell him how excited I was to tell others about Christ. He took one look at me and asked, "What church are you working in, young man?" I tried to avoid his question by telling him about all the hypocrites in churches and the boring sermons. He just stared at me and said, "No work will ever last that is separate from the church of Jesus Christ. Son, get into a real church!"

I walked away with those words weighing heavily on my heart. I had seen so many Bible studies come and go. I had been burned so many times by sour church members who still thought I was a loser. I spent the night tossing, turning, and asking God to show me what to do. Before the night was over, I had my answer. I vowed to get a job in a church so I could give my whole life to telling others about Christ. I couldn't wait to call Diane.

"You had better get a job if you want to get married," she responded, surprised at my announcement. Diane wondered how a guy who would never go to church could get a job working in a church. But I promised her that I would get the job. In the meantime, she kept praying, working, and saving every penny she could.

I arrived back in Ft. Myers in July, as on fire for God as I had ever been. I was determined to give my whole life to serving Him. Somewhere I saw a poster advertising an extension course on the Bible from Stetson University and enrolled immediately.

Dr. Fred Williams, whom the students called Dr. Fred, taught the class. He was visibly surprised when I showed up the first night, long-haired and jean-clad, and I wasn't really sure I'd be welcomed. But as he taught a lesson on the gospels, I was spellbound. I had never heard anyone with such vast intellectual and spiritual knowledge.

After class, he asked me to stay behind for a minute. *This is it,* I thought, *he's going to ask about my high school records and I'm out!*

Instead, Dr. Williams took a personal interest in me and listened to my hopes and dreams. We developed a friendship instantly. He genuinely seemed to care about me, and I was deeply impressed by this godly man. For the first time I looked up to an adult as a role model for my life.

I had no idea then how God would use this man and his vision for Christian education to shape my life and make it possible for me to enter the ministry. I later learned that he was the Director of Missions for the Royal Palm Baptist Association of Southern Baptist Churches in the Ft. Myers and Naples area. But to me, Dr. Fred was a friend.

When I got home that night, I fell on my knees and prayed, "God, I'll go anywhere You want me to go and do anything You want me to do. I just want to serve You." It was a simple and earnest prayer that changed the course of my life.

At 10:00 the next morning, Dr. Fred called and asked if I wanted to give my testimony in a church the next day. "Yes!" I answered instantly, before he could even tell me where it was located.

"It's a small church in Immokalee," he said. "I'll tell them you are coming."

I hung up and immediately called Diane. I told her about my prayer the night before and about Dr. Fred's call that morning. She responded enthusiastically. "I'll go with you," she said. "Pick me up early."

We were two excited kids Sunday morning when we left

Ft. Myers and headed for Immokalee. Suddenly it hit me that we were going to an inland cowboy town where they hated long-haired hippies—and I had long hair!

We arrived at the little country church about 10:30 A.M.— Diane wearing a long granny dress, and I wearing old jeans and a long shirt. I didn't even know to introduce myself to anyone, so we just went in and quietly sat down. At about 11:15 A.M. a man stood up and said, "Dr. Fred promised to send us a preacher, but I guess he couldn't come."

I stood up and shouted, "I'm here!" You should have seen their shock as I walked up to the pulpit. I told them about my life and conversion and sat down. The deacon gave the invitation and three people came forward. I was thrilled, though I was as surprised as they were at the positive response.

The congregation invited me back for the next three weeks and finally asked me to become their interim pastor. On August 15, 1972, just four days before our wedding, I was licensed to preach. In December I was ordained as the full-time pastor of Friendship Baptist Church. Diane and I were newly married, living in Ft. Myers, and commuting to Immokalee. We started when the church had just 17 members and had 117 people saved and baptized the first year, with the attendance reaching 300. We just went door to door, up and down the streets of that little town, telling people about Jesus. It was really all we knew to do.

In the meantime, we opened our home in Ft. Myers for a Bible study to reach street kids. We wanted to help other kids just as other Christians had helped us. Our lives were filled with telling people about Christ and it was wonderful!

As time went on, though, I realized the need for more training. Our congregation was growing into a real church, and I felt inadequate. I continued in the Stetson extension classes and Dr. Fred gave me all the personal attention he could, but I needed more education. And even then I could not shake my burden for my hometown, Ft. Myers. "I'll come back someday, Lord," I promised.

Enrolling in college was not easy for me. After all, I had bad high school grades, no money, and a wife to support. Dr. Fred and I prayed together about what to do. Then he suggested that I check several college catalogs while he checked around for a scholarship.

I finally applied to the Baptist College in Charleston, South Carolina, and was awarded a presidential scholarship and accepted on academic probation. It was a chance, and I decided to take it. We moved to Charleston in 1974 and I started as a full-time student. In addition to my classes, I spent many Sundays sharing my testimony in area churches. To my amazement, people were saved in almost every service.

While I was a student, I also served as the associate pastor of Remount Road Baptist Church. I was maturing in my walk with God and becoming more accustomed to local church ministry. But I never totally divorced myself from my nontraditional roots. Though I had matured and moderated, I was still intolerant of spiritually dead churches, hung up on petty and trivial issues.

Most of the students at my college came from Christian families and traditional churches. They often did not understand how to reach unchurched young people. In many cases they were actually intimidated by them.

"What are you afraid of?" I would often ask other students. "You *have* what these kids need!" But it was always easier for me because I had been on the outside looking in for so long.

I shared my testimony in student revivals, church services, and youth rallies. I also began addressing high school assemblies. I believed God wanted me to be honest about my past and use it to reach out to others who were hurting. They were often willing to open up to me about their past sins and failures. Some had carried the guilt of their past for many years. They wanted forgiveness and release, but did not know how to find it.

After being graduated from the Baptist College, I attended Southwestern Baptist Theological Seminary in Fort Worth,

Texas. There evangelist James Robison influenced me to launch my own evangelistic ministry. After hearing me preach one Sunday night, he offered to write letters to churches and groups recommending me as an evangelist. I began to travel extensively, holding local church crusades and city-wide meetings all over the United States and in several foreign countries. Each time I gave my personal testimony, God blessed it in an unusual way and encouraged me to continue to be honest with others about my past.

Despite the success of my evangelistic ministry, my heart was still with the people back in my hometown in Florida. I had an incredible burden after hearing of Jerry Falwell's Liberty Godparent Homes ministry in his hometown of Lynchburg, Virginia. Ft. Myers was the place where I had been saved and called to preach, and somehow I knew I would return there someday.

When the large Riverside Baptist Church lost its pastor, one of the staff members submitted my name to the pulpit committee for consideration. Although I had preached several revivals there, their initial reaction was very negative. Some of them remembered what I had been like as a kid and couldn't see a drug-using street kid as the pastor of their church.

Despite their hesitations, they agreed to talk to me, though mostly as a courtesy. I shared my burden for Ft. Myers and my vision for the church. Their hearts were moved, and they recommended me to the church, which I pastored for the next three and a half years. It was one thing to travel around the country giving my testimony, but it was a totally different matter to return to my hometown to peach to people who had known me before I was converted.

After a fruitful ministry at Riverside, God clearly led me back into full-time evangelism. Through the years my burden has expanded from my hometown to the whole world. God has opened opportunities for me to preach in city-wide and area-wide crusades all over the world. My ministry now involves working with pastors from several denominations. But in God's providence, having been a local church pastor myself, I have learned how to relate to them.

Preaching the gospel and winning the lost is what God has called me to do. But I realize now that our converts must be channeled into gospel-preaching churches, where they can continue to grow spiritually. New converts need a place of growth and nurture, where God can continue His work in their lives.

Today, as I look back over the past years, I can see that God has been in control all along. When I was a desperate kid, searching for help, He was there to meet me. When I needed direction for my life, He sent people along to give me just what I needed. At every stage, God was there, proving Himself and His love to me.

I am certainly not a psychologist or even a professional counselor. I have no magic answers for life's problems. But I do know a Savior who loves you and can help you overcome whatever is wrong in your life. He can forgive your past, heal your hurts, and give meaning and purpose to your life.

Much of my time is spent ministering to those who have failed in life. Those whose past seems too bad to tell open up to me because they know I can understand. They sense that I care about their hurts, their guilt, and their shame because I have been there too.

When Jesus sent out His disciples to preach, He told them to go out proclaiming His gospel to all who would hear them. If they reject you, He told them, "shake off the dust" and move on to the next town (see Matthew 10:14). In other words, Jesus urged His followers not to be trapped by failure or rejection, but to shake it off and keep moving.

I believe that is exactly what God wants us all to do today as well. You cannot remain a victim of your past forever. Shake it off by God's grace and move on to a life of meaningful service.

Too many people are living like spiritual orphans instead of living like the children of God. Wake up! We have a heavenly Father who loves us and whose grace is sufficient to forgive our sins and overcome our pasts.

I know what God has done for me and I know He can do it for you too. In the chapters that follow are the stories of people whose past trapped them in an emotional prison of self-defeat. In each case God intervened to set them free. He became their Father, and He never intends to let them go. He makes the same offer to you.

# PROBLEMS
# OF
# THE
# PRESENT

## Chapter 4

# Alcohol: America's Favorite Drug

ALLEN NEVER DRANK heavily in high school. Oh, occasionally he had a little too much, but he was usually pretty straight back then. We grew up together in Ft. Myers and knew each other in high school. I'm sure there were times when he thought I would never make it. But I never worried about him. He seemed to have it all together. He was strong, tough, and quiet. Nobody messed with him and he didn't bother anybody else.

Eventually his drunken moods changed from silly to mean. Alcohol made him fighting mad. It lowered his inhibitions and eliminated his self-control so that the anger in him exploded like a bomb. I remember one time when he'd had too much to drink and got into a fight. He beat the other guy senseless and threw him through a window. When he later sobered up, he could hardly remember what had happened.

Allen got out of high school during the height of the Vietnam War. He was drafted and eventually sent to 'Nam. Something snapped inside him while he was there. The pressure of the war aged him and pushed his nerves to a raw edge.

In order to ease the pressure, he began drinking heavily. He would get so wiped out that the other guys would have to carry him back to the barracks, and several times he woke up in an alley with no idea of how he had gotten there. What was worse, he also had no idea of what he had done before he got there.

When he returned home to Ft. Myers after his stint in Vietnam, Allen had become a confirmed alcoholic. He drank heavily every day, and he often mixed cocaine or heroin with his drinks. The effect was devastating on both his mind and his body.

Allen drank to escape. But the world to which he escaped soon became more of a nightmare than the one from which he was running. He vomited excessively, and hallucinated almost daily. His inner world existence soon became his own personal twilight zone, where the real and the unreal merged without distinction.

Like all alcoholics, he told himself, "I can quit anytime if I really want to." But he didn't quit. He kept drinking more and more until he could no longer hold a steady job.

Some people drink to celebrate the good times, and others drink to forget the bad times. Allen did both! In fact, he drank so constantly that the occasion didn't even matter anymore.

Going home is never easy for people like Allen. He had no success story to tell, no war victory to brag about. He just had a lot of pain and bad memories that he wanted to forget. Going back to preach in Ft. Myers was not easy for me either. Ft. Myers was the place where I had made such a mess of my life. But it was also the place where I had come to know Christ and been delivered.

While Allen was in Vietnam, I was in school studying for the ministry. Not only had time and distance separated us, but our lives had also gone in separate directions. When I returned to Ft. Myers to pastor the Riverside Baptist Church, Allen had returned as an alcoholic. We were about as far apart as two people could get.

Despite all that had happened in our lives, I understood what he was going through from my past experiences, and my heart reached out to him. He wasn't used to the idea of my being a pastor and didn't quite know how to handle it. "I can't believe you're a preacher, Jay," he would often say.

"I can't either," I would reply. "But I sure do like it."

"What is there to like about it?" he asked one day.

"I've wanted to talk to you ever since I came back to town," I said. "You look like you're having a tough time of it."

"Yeah, I guess I am," he answered. "But I can handle it."

Allen was in his thirties by now and he was starting to age fast. All he had been through in Vietnam and all he was putting himself through now was taking its toll on him. He even had difficulty trying to smile. His eyes were blurry and his skin was leathery.

"Don't you think it's time to get your life straight?" I asked. "You can't go on like this forever."

"I know," he replied hesitantly. "I've tried to quit, but I always go back to it."

"You're hooked," I said, "and you've got to face it. Nobody can solve this for you."

"You're a preacher. What should I do?"

"Let's start by getting a cup of coffee," I suggested.

We drove to a little place nearby and sat down together to talk and drink coffee.

"Is this supposed to sober me up?" he asked, smiling.

"Not really," I answered, "but it sure beats what you've been drinking!"

As we talked Allen poured his heart out to me about his life of failure and disappointment. He talked at length about his experiences in Vietnam and his inability to handle the horror of it all.

"I guess I'm at the bottom, huh?" he asked.

"Well, you're pretty close to it," I said.

"I really want help, Jay," he announced, looking me straight in the eye, "but I don't know what to do."

Gently and patiently, I began to share my testimony with him. I told him how Christ had delivered me from alcohol and drugs.

"He can do the same thing for you," I said. "You know that beer commercial that says 'you only go around once in life, so grab all the gusto you can'?"

"Yeah, I've seen it," he replied.

"Well, it's a lie!" I exclaimed. "You don't just 'go around once.' You have to face eternity one day and then what is going to happen?"

"I really don't like to think about it," he said.

"Of course you don't," I answered, "because you're not ready for it!"

He looked down for a moment and began to reflect on his life. "Do you think God can really help someone like me?"

"Sure He can," I said. "That's what I'm here for. I'm going to tell you how."

As I presented the gospel to him, Allen sat in rapt attention.

"You're a sinner, man," I told him. "That is why your life is in such a mess. The only way out of this personal hell you have created is to turn your life over to God by confessing your sins, trusting Christ as your Savior, and letting Him take control of you."

We talked for nearly an hour and finally Allen said, "I'm ready, Jay. I want to ask God to forgive me, and I want Christ to come into my life."

We bowed our heads right there in the little restaurant and prayed together. As best as he knew how, Allen gave his life to Christ. "Now what should I do?" he asked.

"We need to go to your place and throw away all the booze you've got," I said. "That will help you make a clean break from it."

As we drove to his apartment, I could see the hope in his eyes. He was happy and buoyant. He seemed relieved and glad that he had done something right for a change.

Allen had tried counseling programs and been to a psychologist. He had tried rehab programs. None of these had worked until he gave his life to Christ. Although he quit "cold turkey," it took a lot of time for his marriage to heal and for him and his wife to communicate freely again. It took time for her to trust him again, but through a support group of caring friends, Allen learned to live a new life. He's had a few setbacks, but those have taught him to trust in God. Today, he is a changed person. He is "a new creation in Christ Jesus," as the Bible promises in 2 Corinthians 5:17.

Allen now volunteers his time to help others find Christ and experience healing through God's transforming power.

## AMERICA'S THIRD LARGEST HEALTH PROBLEM

Alcoholism is America's third largest health problem, following heart disease and cancer. It afflicts ten million people, costs sixty billion dollars annually, and is implicated in 200,000 deaths annually. Alcohol is involved in 50 percent of automobile-related deaths and 67 percent of all homicides. It has ruined countless marriages and broken up millions of homes.[1]

Alcohol is produced by natural fermentation of fruit, grain, or vegetables. This is caused by microscopic one-celled fungi or yeasts. Alcohol is most commonly consumed as beer, wine, or hard liquor. When it is absorbed into the bloodstream, it acts as a depressant on the central nervous system. It slows reflexes and coordination, and affects the thought processes of the brain.[2]

Varying doses of alcohol can produce impulsive behavior, impaired thinking, blurred vision, altered perception, and loss of coordination (or staggering). Effects vary from one person to another. Some become emotional when drunk, while others become aggressive and hostile.[3]

Alcohol poses serious problems for pregnant women and their babies. The National Institute on Alcohol Abuse and Alcoholism has released strong warnings based upon studies that show that pregnant women who take more than two drinks a day run a significant risk of bearing retarded or deformed babies.

Alcohol creates both physical and psychological dependencies. While most alcoholics drink to escape their problems, they create worse problems for themselves by drinking. The physical craving for alcohol is sometimes so great that breaking the bondage requires hospitalization and detoxification (drying out).

Chronic alcoholism causes extensive damage to the brain, liver, pancreas, and nervous system. Cirrhosis of the liver is now the fourth leading cause of death in males age fifty-five to sixty-five. Alcoholics also tend to have higher rates of cancer and heart disease. The average lifespan of a heavy drinker is generally shortened by eleven years.[4]

The cost of alcohol to our society is astronomical. Nearly one-half of all arrests are alcohol related. Ninety percent of all assaults, and sixty percent of all rapes and homicides are committed by persons under the influence of alcohol: 26,000 deaths and 500,000 disabling injuries are caused by drunk drivers each year. In total, nearly 250,000 people die each year from alcohol, its illness, or its related crimes.[5]

## TEENAGE DRINKING

In addition to adult problem drinkers, the National Institute on Alcohol Abuse and Alcoholism estimates that 19 percent of all adolescents, aged fourteen to seventeen, are problem drinkers.[6] That means there are over three million adolescent problem drinkers in America.

An analysis of 100 surveys on teenage drinking conducted between 1941 and 1975 showed the number of high school students who admitted to getting drunk at least once increased 400 percent. Those who admitted to getting drunk *once a week* doubled.[7]

Surveys conducted by the National Institute on Alcohol Abuse and Alcoholism released in 1980 revealed the following information:

- Three out of ten students in grades seven through twelve are problem drinkers, and 58 percent of these are boys.
- Of teens thirteen and younger, 24 percent can be classified as moderate drinkers.

- One in four teenagers reported being drunk *more than four times* during the past year.
- 45.6 percent admitted to being drunk at least once during the past year.
- Nearly 40 percent of all teenage drinkers acknowledged they did their drinking while driving or sitting in a car.
- 70 percent of those teens who acknowledged that they had smoked marijuana rated themselves as heavy drinkers.
- Ironically, only 2.4 percent of all teenage drinkers surveyed saw their drinking pattern as "considerable" or "serious."[8]

Several concepts can be drawn from this information:

1. *Drinking is a serious teenage problem.* The majority of America's teenagers drink alcoholic beverages. Whether they do it for social reasons, in order to join the party, or because of pressure from their friends or depression and escapism, they are still drinking. Eighty-seven percent of all high-school seniors admitted to taking at least one alcoholic drink during their school years. A recent poll of high-school coaches published in *USA Today* presented alcohol as the number one drug of teenagers today.

2. *Teenage drinkers begin early.* Further details of the survey on teenage drinking revealed that 63 percent of the boys and 54 percent of the girls had tried alcohol. Further, 5 percent of seventh grade boys and 4.4 percent of seventh grade girls were already problem drinkers. The greatest increases in drinking came between the seventh and eighth grade for boys and the eighth and ninth grade for girls. Researcher S. L. Englebardt stated, "By the time students reached their final year of school nearly 40 percent of twelfth grade boys and 21 percent of twelfth grade girls had been defined as problem drinkers."[9]

3. *Drinking often leads to drugs.* The vast majority of teenagers who took drugs admitted that they had been alcohol drinkers before they got into drugs and that heavy drinking lowered their resistance to drugs.[10]

4. *Drinking often leads to accidents.* Every year 8,000 teenagers die because of drunk driving. It is the number one killer of young people aged 16 to 21. In commenting on these statistics, Robert Anastas, the founder and director of Students Against Driving Drunk (SADD), stated, "They don't die in single numbers. They die in groups. They die with two or three friends."[11]

5. *Teenagers do not take drinking seriously.* If 87 percent of all teenagers drink alcoholic beverages at some time, and nearly half of them become problem drinkers, why do only 2.4 percent admit they have a drinking problem? The answer is obvious—they don't want to admit it to themselves! This is what makes drinking so dangerous. One drink often leads to another until the drinker is totally out of control. The tragedy is that everyone knows it but him!

## WHY DO KIDS DRINK?

A *Special Report to the U.S. Congress on Alcohol and Health,* prepared by the Secretary of Health, Education, and Welfare in June 1987, cited these influences as the major factors in teenager drinking:

1. *Family and Parents.* Parental pressure was found to be the number one cause of teenage drinking. Parents often encourage their children to drink at home, parties, weddings, anniversaries, holidays, and even family meals. In fact, Robert Zucker, professor of psychology at Michigan State University, has demonstrated that adult problem drinkers will almost always produce children who become problem drinkers.[12]

2. *Peer Pressure.* Adolescents have such a great need for acceptance that they can be persuaded easily by their friends to do just about anything. This quest for acceptance is especially strong during the time when a teenager is striving for greater freedom from the family circle. Woodward comments, "Given the right set of unfortunate circumstances, peer influence can be a volatile agent in determining when a child will first drink.[13]

The fear of rejection is so great in most teenagers that they will give in to peer pressure just to be accepted. This was my biggest downfall as a teenager. I had determined not to drink because of what it had done to my parents, but I was so insecure that I gave in to the pressure of the crowd.

3. *Sociocultural Influences*. Studies have also revealed that certain social groups and ethnic subcultures are more likely to produce problem drinkers because everybody in their social world is doing it. The *Special Report to Congress* revealed that reported cases of alcoholism in America were highest among Eskimos and American Indians. Next highest were whites, then Hispanics and blacks. Orientals claimed the lowest numbers of problem drinkers. Among caucasians, problem drinkers generally came from families with European roots where drinking was a common social expression.[14]

4. *Contextual Influences*. Studies reveal that the youngest child in a family is more likely to become a problem drinker than the oldest child. Patterns of responsibility, maturity, and development may affect the potential of one's vulnerability to alcohol.[15]

5. *Psychological Factors*. Many teens drink to relieve psychological pressure caused by fear, guilt, tension, insecurity, or low self-image. These factors combine to provoke the desire to escape the real world through alcohol. Unfortunately, such pressures especially prey on those who drink alone. They are the ones who are most likely to become serious alcoholics.[16]

6. *Adult Role Models*. The adult culture subtly pressures teenagers to drink in order to appear mature. Seventy percent of all Americans drink some type of alcohol, which impresses young people that drinking denotes adult status. As a result, many teens feel that alcohol is a shortcut to maturity. A five-year study of drinking shown on television programs revealed that viewers were exposed to more than eight alcohol-drinking situations every hour, and that the rate of this activity was rising. All sorts of TV characters drank, except young people.[17] The unconscious message is if you want to grow up, drink.

7. *Advertising Pressure*. The multibillion-dollar-a-year profit of the alcoholic beverage industry enables it to pour mil-

lions of dollars into advertising, which promotes and glamorizes drinking. According to the U.S. Commerce Department, newspapers in 1981 received $95 million in advertising from the beer and wine industry alone, while television received $303 million and magazines received $258 million.[18] Virtually all of this advertising promoted drinking as the "in" thing to do, the source of fun and good times. A skid row drunk would never be used in a beer commercial. On the other hand, the alcoholic beverage industry clearly exploits the masculine ideal by identifying all cool, swinging, mature, athletic, and sensuous males as drinkers of beer, wine, and liquor.

## SYMPTOMS OF ALCOHOLISM

Linda Hindson developed the following checklist for the Virginia Baptist Hospital to help to pinpoint potential drinking problems among teenagers.[19]

| CHECKLIST FOR SYMPTOMS OF ALCOHOLISM | Yes | No |
|---|---|---|
| 1. Do you drink to overcome shyness or to feel more confident? | ☐ | ☐ |
| 2. Are you having money troubles because of your drinking? | ☐ | ☐ |
| 3. Do you ever miss school or work because of your drinking? | ☐ | ☐ |
| 4. Is your drinking giving you a bad reputation? | ☐ | ☐ |
| 5. Are you less ambitious and efficient than when you drank less? | ☐ | ☐ |
| 6. Do you drink to escape from your problems? | ☐ | ☐ |
| 7. Do you drink when you are alone? | ☐ | ☐ |
| 8. Do you have loss of memory during or after your drinking? | ☐ | ☐ |
| 9. Do you need a drink at a different time every day? | ☐ | ☐ |
| 10. Do you drink in the morning? | ☐ | ☐ |
| 11. Has a doctor ever treated you because of your drinking? | ☐ | ☐ |
| 12. Do you make promises to yourself or others about your drinking? | ☐ | ☐ |

13. Do you have to keep drinking once you've started?  ☐  ☐
14. Have you had an accident because of your drinking?  ☐  ☐
15. Do you drink to relieve the painfulness of living?  ☐  ☐
16. Do you have trouble getting rid of cans and bottles?  ☐  ☐
17. Has your drinking affected your health?  ☐  ☐
18. Do you become more moody, jealous, or irritable after your drinking?  ☐  ☐

One YES answer: A warning.
Two YES answers: You probably are an alcoholic.
Three or more YES answers: You are an alcoholic and should find help at once.

No one likes to admit that he or she is an alcoholic, but until you do you will never seek help or treatment. Half-hearted attempts to quit or gradually cut down will only leave you frustrated and defeated.

## GETTING SOBER

There is no simple method for treating alcoholism. The recovery process is complicated and success varies from one person to another. The type of treatment and the stages of withdrawal depend on the seriousness of one's drinking problem.

Three stages of treatment are generally suggested in secular literature:[20]

1. *Management of Acute Intoxication and Withdrawal.* This is generally recommended for those who are saturated with alcohol and will suffer from acute withdrawal symptoms. In order to rid the body of alcohol, the user is generally hospitalized in a detoxification unit and dried out.

2. *Medical Treatment.* Such treatment is designed to deal with the side effects of alcohol—liver, brain, and heart damage. Medical treatment varies with the individual drinker and the length and extent of his habit. Secondary illnesses are treated before the patient is brought into long-term treatment.

3. *Long-Term Treatment.* The final phase of this process is the most difficult because it is designed to alter the alcoholic's long-term behavioral and drinking patterns. The treatment process includes counseling, psychotherapy, family and group support, behavioral and aversion therapy. Behavioral therapy rewards good behavior and aversion therapy punishes bad behavior. One of the oldest and best known self-help groups is Alcoholics Anonymous. While not religious in nature, AA, as it is popularly known, has an excellent cure rate. Coupled with professional counseling and spiritual help, AA can definitely help alcoholics. Al Anon provides a similar source of aid to the families of alcoholics.

But no matter how helpful these treatment procedures may be, they don't have the power to change the individual. Drinking is an internal problem, not an external one. It begins in the habit, character, and moral fabric of one's life. Apart from divine help, most alcoholics are never cured.

4. *Spiritual Conversion.* The greatest solution to the alcohol problem that I have found is personal spiritual conversion. When people give their lives to Christ, they discover what real life is all about. First, God comes to live within the individual through his spiritual rebirth. Secondly, God's Spirit indwells and empowers the believer to live for God. What a person cannot do alone, God can do through the believer.

When Allen surrendered his life to Christ, confessed his alcoholism as sin, and turned to God for help, he found the deliverance he sought. So can you! If you have never received Christ as your personal Savior and turned over your life to Him, do it now. This is the first step toward victory. You may need medical assistance, but remember, the doctor can't keep you sober. Only God can do that.

## STAYING SOBER

Once you've gotten sober, don't give in to the old pressures. Stay away from temptation. Get rid of all of your alcohol. Avoid places where it is bought or sold. Above all, grow spiritually.

That's right! You need to grow into spiritual maturity. Dealing with hurt, anger, and guilt will remove the causes of depression, which often drive you to drink. When you are down, call a friend—don't sit alone, sulking. Get out and start meeting the needs of others. Get your attention off of yourself and your problems and focus on helping someone else.

1. *Don't Give Up.* No one ever said this would be easy. You may have struggles along the way, but keep on going. When things get tough, turn to God for help. When you need Him most, He will always be there to help you. When the pressure is on, live by faith in His promises. When the bottom falls out, keep on praying. He will never give up on you; don't you give up on Him. Find a Christian support group you can rely on at any hour.

2. *Don't Quit.* Quitters are never winners. They never succeed because they take the easy way out. Keep praying, reading, serving, growing. God's work in you is a life-long process. The Bible says, "Being confident of this very thing, that He who has begun a good work in you will complete it until the day of Jesus Christ" (Philippians 1:6).

3. *Don't Go Back.* Remember, alcohol was ruining your life. It isn't worth going back to it. Teach yourself to hate it. Face it for what it really is—poison! You can never build a worthwhile life as long as you are hooked on alcohol. When you get it out of your life, you are truly free to live life to the fullest. I used to be so fearful that I was going to miss out on something in life, and I kept looking for that 'something' in a bottle. Believe me, it isn't there.

4. *Don't Look to Others.* Even though God uses people in your life for your good, people will fail and let you down. That is why the author of Hebrews wrote, "Looking unto Jesus the author and finisher of our faith" (Hebrews 12:2). Jesus is the only one who never fails. He is the same yesterday, today, and forever.

One of the greatest promises in scripture is found in the words of our Lord, who said, "In the world you will have tribulation; but be of good cheer, I have overcome the world" (John 16:33). Our ultimate success has been guaranteed by our Savior. He has already conquered sin and death for us. Because we are in Him and He is in us, we are assured of victory. Thus the Bible promises us: "We are more than conquerors through Him who loved us" (Romans 8:37). Once we realize that He is the victor, we can enjoy the conflict because we are assured of the victory.

You *can* live a successful Christian life because Jesus Christ lives within you. As you live by faith in Him and walk in the power of His Spirit, you can overcome the world, the flesh, and the devil. Never underestimate His power. Instead, like the apostle Paul, you can say, "I can do all things through Christ who strengthens me" (Philippians 4:13).

## Chapter 5

# Drugs: Hiding Behind the Chemical Curtain

DON WAS A nineteen-year-old college student when I first met him at one of my crusades in Atlanta. He was dressed in a sweat shirt, jeans, and deck shoes with no socks. He had long sandy hair, an earring in one ear, and he was obsessed with drugs.

"I heard the announcement about your assembly tomorrow morning at the high school," he said to me after the evening service. "I'll be there," he added almost pleadingly.

It was not unusual for visitors to attend the high-school assemblies, but it was unusual for a college student who obviously had problems to be willing to come to a high school to get some answers.

As we drove to the school the next morning, I wondered if he would really be there. Some kids from the crusade church, who were excited about our being in their school, met our group on the sidewalk. After talking together for a few minutes, I asked one of the students how to find the principal's office and then went inside.

A relatively conservative school, with neat, clean rooms and carpeted hallways, the kids were typical of suburban Atlanta. Most of them considered themselves to be ordinary American teenagers, but many of them were reported to have serious problems with drugs or alcohol.

As we walked through the maze of kids in the hallways, I

59

saw the principal standing outside his office, waving at me vigorously.

"We are really glad you're here, Jay," he said. "I hope you can help these kids. Some of them really need it."

"Well, I'm glad to be here. I once was just like many of them."

We stepped into his office for a moment to talk about the nature of the assembly. I assured him that I had done over 2,000 assemblies in public schools and would not say anything to violate the restrictions on religion in the public schools.

"I want to keep the door open so you will have me, or somebody like me, back in the future," I explained. "I am going to speak to them simply from the standpoint that I know what they are going through. I'm not going to preach to them, but I am going to tell them what alcohol and drugs can do to ruin their lives."

I love giving assemblies because it gives me a chance to stay in tune with where the kids really are in life. I've seen just about everything in our nation's high schools, from kids passing drugs in the hallways to guys smoking pot in the restrooms.

At ten o'clock the announcement came over the public address system about the assembly. Immediately hundreds of teenagers began filing down the hallways to the gym. Some were toting their books, others were talking excitedly about the assembly, and still others plodded along lazily with bored looks on their faces. These kids were not rebellious. If anything, they were apathetic.

"I wonder what this one's all about?" somebody right behind me asked.

"Have you ever heard this guy speak?" I asked him, without identifying myself.

"No, but he'd better be good or I'm going to sleep," the teenager responded.

As the principal introduced me to speak, I jumped up, turned, smiled at my premature critic, and walked to the microphone in the center of the floor.

When I do an assembly, I have no props. It is just me, the mike, and the kids. I begin by telling my life story. I tell about my dad's leaving when I was six and about my stepfathers and all the problems they had with drinking. I relate the part about my teenage drinking and drug problem. And finally, I talk about the battle for the mind and the battle for the body. I deal with drugs, alcohol, teenage sex, pregnancy, and abortion.

Although I can't share the gospel in a public school assembly, I do let them know that I was delivered from drugs and alcohol and that I found the "way of escape." I usually end by saying, "Don't blow your life; the best is yet to come!"

Afterward hundreds of kids poured off the bleachers and bombarded me with questions and comments. Some wanted to argue, but most wanted to thank me for coming. Some were looking for help and promised to come to the crusade service that night to hear more. As the crowd began to disperse, I noticed Don, standing alone, quietly crying.

"I need to talk to you," he said when he got me alone. "I'm really into drugs heavy, and I need help. In fact, I'm carrying $100 worth of crack on me right now."

"Why don't we step outside," I suggested.

As we walked down the hallway, he tried to regain his composure. I said good-bye to the principal, and Don and I walked to the car together.

"Can we talk right here?" he asked.

"Sure," I replied as I leaned up against the car.

Don looked down at the sidewalk for a minute and then looked up at me with a pleading look in his eyes. "This isn't easy to talk about," he said. "My dad is pretty well known, and I don't want to embarrass him."

"You probably already have," I suggested gently. "Telling me isn't going to make it any worse, and it could really help."

"You're right," he said. "It all started in high school. I started smoking pot when I was fifteen. Eventually someone introduced me to cocaine, and it really blew me away. I started snorting the powder, and then someone showed me how to use crack. I'm into it really bad."

"Do you really want help, Don?" I asked as I reached out my hand to steady his shaking shoulders.

"Yes, I do," he said. "I heard you last night at the crusade. I want to believe that God can deliver me from drugs, but I'm scared."

"What are you scared of?" I asked.

"I'm afraid I won't be able to live it," he replied. "I want to turn my life over to Christ. But what if nothing changes?"

"Why don't you leave that up to God?" I asked. "In Romans 10:13, God promises to save all who call upon Christ as Savior."

I quoted the verse to him and asked him if he would be willing to trust Christ personally to come into his life, save him, forgive him, and deliver him from drugs.

"Yes," he said simply and firmly.

"Then let's pray right here and ask Him to do it," I suggested.

We bowed our heads and prayed together. With tears streaming down his face, Don prayed out loud to receive Christ as his personal Savior. He confessed his sins and his own helplessness and called on God to deliver him from drugs.

When we finished, he looked up at me and said, "I should have done that a long time ago." We smiled at each other and shook hands. I knew in my heart that he understood what he had done. Don reached into his jacket pocket and handed me his drugs.

"Here, take these," he insisted. "I won't be needing them anymore. I'll see you again tonight at the crusade." We shook hands again and he walked off toward his car.

That night, Don's father approached me after the service and thanked me for talking to his son that morning. "He's already a different kid," his father insisted. "I just can't believe the change that has come over him."

Before the week was over, the entire family had been converted to Christ. They began to pray together and attend church together. They all reached out to Don to help support him through his physical withdrawal from drugs. They cried together, prayed together, and laughed together.

As his mind began to clear, Don began helping others who were dependent on drugs to experience the deliverance he had come to know in Christ. In the years that followed he went on to school, married a Christian girl, and today, he has a significant ministry himself.

## WHO USES DRUGS?

In my earlier book, *Drugs and Drinking* (Thomas Nelson, revised edition, 1985), I stated that there is no single cause or set of conditions that clearly leads to drug abuse.[1] Instead, people abuse drugs for different reasons. But there are three basic types of drug users:

1. *Occasional Users.* Teenagers as well as adults belong in this category. Housewives who take diet pills to pep them up with extra energy; college students who use amphetamines to stay up all night studying for exams; executives who use alcohol or tranquilizers to soothe their pressures; even habitual smokers—all are occasional users.

2. *Thrill Seekers.* Teenagers or college students who are seeking a thrill from drugs compose this group. Some are only weekend users or party people—they get high to have a good time. But many of these social drug users become seriously hooked and cannot quit.

3. *Addicts.* The addict's, or junkie's, entire life revolves around drugs. His or her dependence on drugs—both psychologically and physically—is so great that he or she cannot function without them. Addicts usually cannot perform as they should at school or on the job.

## WHY DO KIDS TURN TO DRUGS?

The following are five basic reasons teenagers turn to drugs.

1. *Pressure.* Many young people begin using drugs because of peer pressure. They are preoccupied with social acceptance and will do almost anything to gain the approval of other teens. My own early life was a good example of this. As early as the seventh grade, I gave into peer pressure to drink. The crowd

became my god and determined my lifestyle. Any weak-willed teenager can give in to the pressure to follow the crowd, despite the consequences.

Some psychologists call this tendency to follow the crowd the herd instinct.[2] An unconscious, automatic reflex, this instinct drives us to want to be part of a group for security purposes. This drive for social acceptance and personal affiliation is especially strong in teenagers, who are already undergoing physiological changes.

I am convinced that it takes more courage to stand alone than to follow the crowd. All of the trouble I got into as a teenager came from my following the crowd. When our gang did something wrong, we *all* did it and everyone joined in.

2. *Escape.* Many young people are looking for an escape from the problems of life. They want to wave the magic wand of drugs and have an easy solution to their restlessness, alienation, pain, or neglect.

Teens turn on to escape the hassles of home, school, dating, friends, and even self. Most psychologists view adolescence as the most stressful period in human development.[3] The adolescent must adjust quickly to vast changes, which occur rapidly and without warning in his or her life.

Self-acceptance is one of the major problems in a teenager's life. Many teens have never learned to accept themselves. They feel lonely, unloved, and depressed, and they believe drugs will provide an escape from all that is wrong in their world. But drug abuse only makes the problems worse because it results in a vicious cycle of ups and downs that leaves the user trapped in a chemical prison and emotionally unstable.

3. *Availability.* Drugs are everywhere today, and most kids know how to get them, which makes them a constant temptation to the average teenager. A recent Gallup Poll indicated that 81 percent of high-school teens indicated that marijuana was readily available in their school.[4] As many as 60 percent of high-school seniors have acknowledged using marijuana.

Not only do teens have easy access to drugs, but our affluent society helps them to be able to afford the drugs as well.

These are not only "fast times" on the high school campuses, but also, as one magazine calls it, "high times."[5]

4. *Curiosity.* An Arizona-based drug education program recently reported that 70 percent of drug-using teenagers nationally, and 90 percent of those in Arizona, listed curiosity as the main reason they began to take drugs. "I wanted to see a TV melt before my eyes," one girl admitted.[6]

Many teens turn to drugs for a new experience. Some have their curiosity aroused by music which incorporates drug experiences into the songs. Others have their curiosity stimulated by the stories of friends who have tried to get high. Still others are influenced by television programs, movies, and videos which deal with drugs and drug users.

5. *Emptiness.* The reason so many people *stay* on drugs is because of the inner emptiness they feel. We are experiencing a bankruptcy of the spirit in America today. An empty person doesn't know *who* he is, *why* he is here, or *where* he is going. He lacks purpose, goals, or direction. He is like a ship adrift without a destination.

The breakup of the home and the breakdown in morality are further symptoms of the void within our lives. Even our great social institutions—home, church, and school—are crumbling around us.

Another evidence of the emptiness in teenagers is their *restlessness*. I always had to be on the go, the music turned up full blast. I quickly developed an "anything-is-better-than-this" philosophy about life. Most teenagers today never heard of Janis Joplin, but the words to her song still ring true: "Freedom's just another word for nothing left to lose." She took her life by drug overdose. Jimmy Hendrix, Jim Morrison, and even Elvis Presley met similar fates.

The life of a drug user is like a skydiver's jump: it thrills for a while, but without a parachute, it's deadly.

## WHAT KIND OF DRUGS ARE POPULAR?

1. *Marijuana.* The abuse of marijuana is the most common drug problem in America today. Marijuana is a drug

found in the flowery tops and leaves of the Indian hemp plant *(cannabis sativa)*. It contains THC (tetrahydrocannabinal) resin, which is stronger if the plant is grown in a tropical climate.

The drug is popularly called pot, tea, hemp, grass, or weed. To be used as a drug, its leaves and flowers are cut, dried and crushed into small pieces. The grassy-looking product is then rolled into homemade cigarettes, called joints. It may also be smoked in a pipe or baked into food.

Marijuana produces a mild high, which is why most users think it is a safe drug. However, it may be refined or mixed in any one of several ways. Today's marijuana is generally much more potent than that used in the 1960s and early 1970s.

Marijuana smoke affects the user after about fifteen minutes and lasts from two to five hours. The THC content of the plant determines the mind-altering effect it may have on a given individual. Sometimes a particular batch is weak, so pushers doctor it with other chemicals rather than lose money. This results in "trash," a low-grade form of pot. Because of this practice, many teenagers end up with damaging chemicals in their bodies.

General marijuana use slows the brain's decision-making capacity and distorts the user's sense of time and distance. The National Institute on Drug Abuse has sponsored over one thousand experimental projects, finding that marijuana impairs learning, speech, and memory, reduces the ability to drive or fly, and has negative effects on heart rate, lung capacity, and reproductive organs.[7]

2. *Cocaine*. Once called the "yuppie" or "rich man's" drug, because of the exorbitant cost, cocaine is now easily available to all ages and financial classes because of "crack" cocaine. Crack is easy to manufacture, thus less expensive and more abundant. Cocaine is a central nervous system stimulant that has become one of our nation's most popular drugs. It is a powerful psychoactive drug that produces excitement, restlessness, and an intense sense of energy and euphoria. It raises blood pressure and increases respiration. Athletes particularly

like crack because it enables them to get "up" quickly for a big game.

Cocaine can be snorted, taken intravenously, or smoked from a freebase solid. Its popularity is due to its quick high, brief hangover, and the fact that it leaves no traceable marks. The user often feels alert, witty, and exciting. However, the deaths due to drug-induced heart attack by several key athletes, such as Len Bias, have caused a national reaction against the drug. Nevertheless, nearly a thousand people a day call the national cocaine hotline (1-800-COCAINE).

"Crack" is the popular term for freebase cocaine, which is made by adding an alkali and solvent to cocaine. This process is generally accomplished by heating ether or lighter fluid, or by adding baking soda and ether to street cocaine. A purified cocaine base, which is smoked in a pipe or sprinkled on marijuana, results. It is rapidly absorbed into the lungs and carried to the brain in a few seconds. The brief euphoria is usually followed by a feeling of restlessness and irritability. Several deaths have been reported from the increased blood pressure and heart rate which result from using crack. Respiratory failure often occurs as the entire cardiovascular system is devastated by the rapidly constricting blood vessels.

Regular users report a total preoccupation with the drug, which leads to a loss of energy, insomnia, loss of sex drive, and irregular heart rate. The initial sense of indestructibility gives way to depression, which inevitably leaves the user wanting another hit of coke.

An addictive drug produces three basic conditions: 1) compulsion, 2) loss of control, 3) continued use of the drug despite adverse effects. According to Dr. Gabriel Nahas of Columbia University, cocaine has all these characteristics and more.[8]

3. *LSD*. The most potent psychedelic drug is lysergic acid diethylamide (LSD). The substance comes from ergot, the fungus that spoils rye grain. The acid itself is often used to cure headaches, but when it is converted to the liquid or powder LSD, it has extreme mind-altering powers. Popularly known as

acid, LSD is 200 times stronger than cocaine. A dose of fifty micrograms (the size of the head of a pin) can put the user on a trip for up to sixteen hours.

LSD exists in both liquid and powder form and is color-less, tasteless, and odorless. Many users put liquid LSD on sugar cubes, aspirin, crackers, or even cookies. One of the as-tonishing properties of LSD is the instant and lasting high one can get from a small amount. One drop of LSD can make 500 people high. Once it gets into the bloodstream and reaches the brain cells, it can last for hours.

Some doctors prefer to categorize LSD as a hallucinogen because its mind-altering properties cause hallucinations and temporary insanity. Others prefer to call it a psychedelic be-cause it produces psychedelic experiences and induces states of self-transcendence and mystical unity. This has always made it popular with certain mystical religions.

4. *Mescaline and Peyote.* These are organic drugs that come from cacti. Mescaline causes hallucinations approxi-mately one hour after being taken and the trips last five to ten hours. These drugs are not physically addictive, but they cause psychological dependence (habituation). Dealers often sell bad acid (LSD) batches laced with "trash" chemicals such as mesca-line or peyote, which yield more potent, more dangerous chem-icals.

5. *Psilocybin.* This substance is found in a certain type of mushroom and is chemically related to LSD. The effects on the user are similar to mescaline and last about six hours. Psilo-cybin may cause dizziness, vomiting, hallucinations, or deep paranoia. Many users actually develop an inordinate fear of dying.

6. *PCP (Angel Dust).* A relatively new and popular drug, PCP was originally sold legally under the trade name Sernyl℗ and used as an anesthetic. It was outlawed for human con-sumption after 1965 because of its severe hallucinogenic ef-fects. PCP is a white crystalline powder that can be smoked, injected, or taken orally. Back-street chemists mix PCP with LSD or sell it as mescaline or psilocybin. Most teenagers falsely

assume these are softer, milder drugs, never realizing they are often laced with LSD.

PCP causes double vision, dizziness, vomiting, convulsive seizures, memory loss, depression, and even suicidal and homicidal tendencies. Overall, it produces a "state of nothingness" in the users and leaves them unaware of their behavior while under its influence. Approximately one hundred kids die each year from the side effects of PCP.

7. *Sniffing Solvents.* Many teenagers try to get high by sniffing glue, paint thinner, gasoline, cleaning fluid, polish remover, or aerosols through plastic bags. The high lasts for five minutes to one hour. The user becomes dizzy, drowsy, silly, and loses all inhibitions. Many teens die from heart attack, asphyxiation, or lead poisoning from this supposedly harmless practice. Still others suffer irreparable brain damage and blood abnormalities.

8. *Stimulants.* These are popularly called uppers and are even used to attempt to cure depression. The most common stimulants are amphetamines such as those used in diet pills. Methamphetamine is chemically related but when injected into the veins produces an incredible "rush." Its popular names are speed, meth, and crystal. Constant users are often called speed freaks. This is the drug that took such a devastating toll on my own life as a teenager. It produces incredible extremes that leave the user up and down and craving more. It becomes the user's social crutch until he feels he can't live without it.

9. *Sedatives.* These are drugs that relax the central nervous system. Popularly called downers, these barbiturates act as depressants. They are usually taken as capsules, and properly prescribed they are not dangerous. But taken irrationally and in heavy doses, they can cause brain damage, respiratory damage, cardiac arrest, and even death. The vulnerability of this drug is that it is highly addictive. Many people, for example, become so hooked on sleeping pills that they cannot get to sleep without them. Every year barbiturates kill more adults than any other drug.

10. *Heroin.* This narcotic is a member of the opium family

and is derived from morphine. Heroin is a white, odorless, crystalline powder. Popularly known as "smack" or "junk," it is sold on the streets illegally for about ten dollars a bag. Heroin addicts are the worst junkies of all because their lives become totally absorbed by their addiction.

Heroin is usually injected intravenously (mainlining) with a hypodermic needle. The heroin itself is measured in a teaspoon, dissolved in water, heated (cooked), and drawn into the needle. In addition to its severely addictive tendencies, the practice of sharing common needles has now spread AIDS to over half the heroin users in America. Thus, this deadly drug is now double indemnity.

## HOW DO KIDS GET HOOKED?

The casual drug user goes through four basic stages of drug abuse that lead to chemical dependency:

1. *Experimental Use.* Most teens began experimenting with drugs because of curiosity or peer pressure. Some may never go beyond the experimental stage, but far too many become regular users. If you have never experimented with drugs, don't start. If you have started, stop now!

2. *Regular Use.* A pattern of regular drug use, coupled with adverse behavioral changes, can indicate dependency. Regular users often become apathetic about life: their grades drop; their companions change; they drop out of sports or activities; and they feel guilt and remorse, which often leads to more drug use.

3. *Daily Preoccupation.* When more and more of your time and energy is spent on assuring a steady supply of drugs, you are hooked. You have established a pattern of daily usage, and your attempts to quit drugs quickly fail because you are at the point of complete dependency. If you really want to quit, seek help now. Don't wait!

4. *Dependency.* By now the user is generally taking drugs several times a day. Abusers at this stage are generally unable to distinguish between normal and abnormal behavior. Drug in-

toxication is a normal daily occurrence and is anticipated by the chemically dependent user. He or she views the high as normal and will do almost anything to maintain it. Rational and moral arguments usually fail to dent the chemical delusion at this point. In most cases, only professional detoxification can help.[9]

## HOW CAN I QUIT?

In order to quit, you must want to quit. Until you desire to get off drugs, you will keep on excusing yourself for taking them. Follow these steps.

1. *Face your problem honestly.* Stop pretending you have it under control and admit you need help. Talk to your parents, your pastor, or a youth counselor. Don't just talk to other kids. Get some real help from people who care.

2. *Admit you are hooked.* Stop trying to cut down. The only way out is to give up your habit totally—make a complete break from it. Begin by admitting to yourself and others just how seriously hooked you are.

3. *Accept personal responsibility.* Don't blame your problem on your parents or anyone else. Take responsibility for what has happened. You started it and you must end it. Make a clean and total break with drugs. Flush them or throw them away so you can't go back for them.

4. *Stay away from temptation.* Avoid people who are using drugs and places where they are being used. Don't put yourself in a place of temptation. Get away from the problem and stay away from the source of temptation.

5. *Quit looking for an easy way out.* There is no simple, magical cure. There are no nonharmful synthetic drugs that can get you unhooked. Doctors, hospitals, psychiatrists, and hypnotists cannot help you. They can provide relief, but they can't make you want to quit—you have to decide that for yourself. Sure there are painful withdrawals, but you can take it! The result will be worth the price you have to pay.

6. *Give yourself to God.* He is the only one who can cure

you. Nothing is impossible with Him. Put your confidence in His Word. Jesus said, "You shall know the truth, and the truth shall make you free" (John 8:32). Confess Christ as your Savior and turn your life over to Him (see Romans 10:13). Then start living the new life God promises to give you (see 2 Corinthians 5:17).

## Chapter 6

# Sex: Our National Pastime

SEXUAL ADDICTION CAN be just as enslaving as alcohol or drugs. Those who are caught in a web of sexual promiscuity or homosexuality often feel helpless to deliver themselves. Attempts at repentance often end in failure, with the victim going right back to sexual sin.

I met Gary in a crusade in Mississippi. He was in his forties, married, and had two children, but he had been an active homosexual most of his adult life. He had a thin, drawn face, and he shifted his eyes continually as he talked to me.

"My wife doesn't know anything about this," he confessed. "I want help, but I always seem to go back to it."

"Have you ever really made a clean break from it?" I asked.

"No," he replied, "not really."

He explained to me that he had tried everything from having electric shock therapy and medication to asking a priest to exorcise demons out of him.

He seemed distraught as he explained the guilt and shame that bound him.

"I can't trust anyone," he said. "I don't even know who I am anymore."

He was so deep into this sin that it had twisted his own identity. He was desperately seeking help, and I knew what could set him free.

"Gary," I said, "I too was once bound like you are, only in my case it was drugs that held me captive. I had to come to the end of myself before I was willing to let God set me free."

"But you're a preacher," he said.

"Well, I haven't always been one," I replied. "I know what you're going through."

"Can you help me?"

"No, but I can tell you who can." I began to explain to him what it meant to turn his life over to Christ and ask Him for forgiveness and deliverance. His eyes began to fill with hope.

"Can God really set me free?" he asked.

"Sure He can," I answered confidently. "It won't be easy, but it can happen." I had to be honest with Gary. Homosexuality is a strong bondage of the flesh. The urge can be as strong as any addictive drug, and it may always be a temptation of the mind.

We talked for some time before he finally bowed his head in prayer and confessed his sin to God. As he prayed, I could sense the relief he was experiencing in his soul. His words were simple, clear, and sincere. I told him it would be necessary to make a clean break with his sinful lifestyle. "You need to admit this to your wife," I said. "She needs to help you get through this, but she can't do it if you aren't honest with her."

"Will you go with me to tell her?" he asked.

"Yes, of course," I replied.

The next days were not easy ones for Gary, but he began to make progress immediately. His wife, Jayne, was hurt deeply and couldn't understand this lifestyle he had hidden for so long. She felt as though *she* had failed. Although this was a normal first response for the spouse of a homosexual, she had not, in fact, failed. The sin of homosexuality is bondage of the flesh and of the spirit: "For we do not wrestle against flesh and blood, but . . . against powers . . . against spiritual hosts of wickedness" (Ephesians 6:12).

Through hours of talking, crying, and listening, they decided to make their marriage work. Jayne thought their sex life had been fine but very infrequent. Gary admitted his neglect was caused by homosexual affairs.

As we counseled together for the next several days, we talked about their hurts and fears. Gary opened up about when and where he had gotten involved with homosexuality, and Gary and Jayne began to pray and talk together every day. Their relationship grew as it never had before. They helped each other through tough times, and Gary finally made a complete break with his past. He gave up the old friends that had dragged him down. He stayed away from places where he knew he would be tempted.

Unlike Gary, who had been involved with many men, Don only struggled with one. Don was a muscular, blond-haired surfer from Miami, the only child in a wealthy and prominent family. Although women were attracted to him, he never related well to them. He never could seem to find words to express himself to them.

Eventually, Don became involved with Tony. Most of the time Don was straight, but whenever Tony was around the two would engage in homosexual activities.

"I guess I never should have started it in the first place," Don admitted. "But now I can't seem to get away from him."

Don and I met at a high-school assembly in the Miami area. He didn't look like a homosexual, nor did he talk like one, which showed me that it's a mistake to try to stereotype homosexuals.

"But I am one," he insisted.

"That all depends," I suggested.

"What do you mean?"

"Well, it is a matter of opinion as to how one's homosexuality is determined," I said. "I look at it this way: you are only a homosexual because of what you have done, not because of what you are." I went on to explain to Don that we are all sinners by nature and that his sin was no less or no greater than anyone else's sin. "I don't buy the idea that people are born homosexual. I believe it is a learned practice which can be unlearned if you are willing to reject it."

"Can you help me?" he asked desperately.

I told him how I had been molested as a child and the guilt, shame, and fear I had experienced. "But that didn't make me a homosexual," I told him. "I hated it and repudiated it. I never consciously desired it."

"That's how I feel," Don said. "I don't want to keep doing it."

"Then quit!" I said abruptly. "Stop seeing Tony. Get away from the temptation. Stop putting yourself down and giving in to it."

As we talked, Don, who was already a church member and professing Christian, prayed with me and confessed his sin and weak will to God. He asked for His forgiveness and His power to help him overcome this sin in his life.

For Don, the change came quickly. He made a clean break from Tony and immediately began to show signs of spiritual growth. The guilt he had known was replaced by confident expectation and hope. Although he had struggles with sin, he became actively involved in his church youth group and, in time, became a spiritual leader in his church. He stopped letting the past defeat him. He *shook off the dust* and went on to a new and better life.

Heterosexuals, as well as homosexuals, struggle with sexual addiction, which is as binding as any other physical addiction. Nancy was a married woman in her early thirties. She had three school-aged children and a husband named Tom, who loved her dearly. But she had become involved in an adulterous relationship shortly after they were married.

"I was bored and restless," she confessed. "I didn't want to do anything wrong. I just wanted some attention."

After several months of being involved in the affair, she finally broke off the relationship, thinking she could get herself together and go on as though nothing had happened. But in time, she and Tom drifted further apart emotionally.

"We went through all the motions of being married," she said, "but there was a barrier and I knew it."

Eventually, she became sexually involved with several men. Each time she tried to tell herself not to let it get started, but then she gave in almost compulsively.

"It happened so many times that it all became a blur in my

mind," she said. "I guess I really didn't want to think about what I was doing. But every time I tried to quit one relationship, I'd get into another."

"Have you ever committed your life to Christ?" I asked her.

"I went to church as a child, but I feel so lost and far away from God now."

"That is because you are far away from Him," I said. "You have been living as if He doesn't exist, hoping you will not be held accountable for your behavior."

As my wife, Diane, and I talked with Nancy, we could see the guilt and confusion in her eyes. After a while she began to cry uncontrollably.

"How could I let this happen to me?" she asked repeatedly.

"It doesn't matter how it got started," I said. "You are hooked on illicit sex and you've got to break the habit."

I shared with her how hopelessly hooked on drugs I once was. I told her all the excuses I had tried to give myself.

Then I said, "I finally had to face the fact that I was the problem and that I had to change."

I told her what Christ had done for me and what He could do for her. We all prayed together and asked God to forgive her and set her free. We went through all the steps of breaking an addiction and set up regular counseling and accountability for her in her community.

Nancy repented and broke with her secret sinful lifestyle. Today she is a glowing Christian with grown teenagers. She and her husband are actively involved as youth sponsors at their local church. God has honored her commitment.

## TEMPTATION BEGINS IN THE MIND

Although sexual sin certainly involves physical activity, it actually begins in one's mind. Whether one is driven by lust or loneliness does not matter. The Bible says, "For as he thinks in his heart, so is he" (Proverbs 23:7).

Men often battle with *impulsive* lust, while women are more likely to battle with *selective* lust. Men are vulnerable to lust of the eyes, whereas women are more vulnerable to the lust of the flesh. Men often fall into temptation seeking physical pleasure, whereas women fall into temptation seeking emotional pleasure. Whether she craves his attention or he craves her body, the results are usually the same: an uncontrollable affair which leads to hurt, bitterness, and anguish.

Both men and women are vulnerable to lustful desires. People who spend time fantasizing about old lovers or watching movies about sexual involvements are programming their minds for potential adultery. Emotional magnetism combined with physical attraction produce a catalytic effect that heads two people straight for trouble.

In his powerful and helpful book *Running the Red Lights*, Charles Mylander observed:

> Ever since God created male and female, each sex has found something fascinating about the other. At its best, this powerful attraction leads to some of life's profound joys. . . . At its worst, misused sex leads to ugly wounds and lasting scars.[1]

Then he warned, "Sooner or later almost every Christian struggles with sexual temptation. Very few escape this battle without a skirmish or two. Some fight the war every day."[2]

The Bible is filled with examples of sexual sinners, like the woman taken in adultery (see John 8:1–11) who came to Christ, was forgiven, and was set free. But scripture is also filled with examples of believers who battled sexual temptation.

With Abraham, it was bigamy. To this day, nations are at odds because of it.

With David, it was adultery. His own sons turned against him.

With Samson, it was compulsive lust. He was humiliated, became blind, and eventually died.

With Hosea's wife, Gomer, it was a series of illicit affairs. Their marriage was a disaster.

With some Corinthians, it was homosexuality and incest.

Anyone can fall into sexual sin innocently or deliberately. One poet called it "the innocent beginning of all my sinning."[3] But once it starts, it gets out of control fast. Conversations turn to sexual frustration and marital unhappiness. Casual touching leads to longer embraces. At first, each would insist nothing is wrong, but you can tell you are going over the edge when you can hardly wait to do it again. In time, admiration and attention turn to excitement and lust. Pretty soon you find yourself going all the way.

J. Allen Peterson summarized the process that takes one from lustful thought to illicit action like this: "Our minds feed the fantasy, the fantasy creates the emotions, and the emotions scream for the actual experience."[4]

## PUTTING ON THE BRAKES BEFORE IT'S TOO LATE

Deal with temptation when it first arises. Don't play around with it, simply hoping it will go away. Ever since the beginning of the human race, men and women have faced temptation. In fact, the Bible reminds us: "No temptation has overtaken you except such as is common to man" (1 Corinthians 10:13). Temptation is unique to no one. It is a universal problem.[5]

One of the major reasons people cannot deal effectively with temptation is their refusal to face the real source of their temptation, themselves.

1. *Don't blame God or the devil*. The easiest way to avoid responsibility regarding our own lives is to blame everything on someone else. This is the "devil-made-me-do-it" mentality or the "why-is-God-doing-this-to-me?" attitude. James 1:13 tells us that God cannot tempt anyone, but we are tempted by our own desires. The desire itself, however, is not the sin: "when desire has conceived, it gives birth to sin" (James 1:15).

2. *Admit your weakness*. Honestly confess your weakness to God. Trust Him to forgive and cleanse you. Believe that God can make a difference in your life. Acknowledging your sin is not a sign of weakness, but a sign of courage. The scripture

warns, "If I regard iniquity in my heart, the Lord will not hear" (Psalm 66:18).

3. *Be willing to change*. Before you can ever change your behavior, you have to be willing to change. As long as you keep making excuses for failure, you will never find deliverance and freedom. Tell God, "I'm willing to do whatever I have to do to be what you want me to be."

4. *Make a 100-percent commitment*. There must come a point where you are disgusted with how you've been living and are determined to go all the way for God. He is the source of deliverance. Don't hold anything back. Half-hearted commitment will not work.

5. *Keep renewing your strength*. The scripture teaches that you are to be "transformed by the renewing of your mind" (Romans 12:2). Keep cleansing your thoughts by meditating on God's Word. Jesus overcame temptation by quoting and trusting the Word of God. Spiritual renewal works like physical exercise. Keep at it!

6. *Trust God for the victory*. He is faithful to preserve us in temptation. While the trials may come our way, He will see to it that we are not tempted above our ability to resist (see 1 Corinthians 10:13). When the pressure comes, turn to Him for help. The Bible says, "Resist the devil and he will flee from you" (James 4:7).

7. *Take the "way of escape."* The Bible promises that there is always a way of escape from every temptation (1 Corinthians 10:13). Find it and take it. Get away from the source of temptation. If you are especially enticed by a certain person, don't let yourself get too close. Stay away from enticing settings and situations as well.

## WHAT IF IT'S TOO LATE?

What if you have already gone too far? Then don't go any further.

Once you have gone too far, there are going to be consequences, but that doesn't mean it's too late to get out of a mess. The ideal is not to get involved in the first place. But if you have already gone beyond that barrier, turn around before it's too late.

One sexual involvement doesn't make you a sexual addict for life. Quit now. You may have experimented with homosexual or heterosexual sin, but that does not make you a confirmed homosexual or a confirmed adulterer.

When Jesus talked to the woman at the well in John 4, he recognized that she had been married five times and was then living adulterously with another man. Instead of condemning her, He offered pardon, forgiveness, and a new life.

Charles Mylander observed that "if neither the man nor the woman puts on the brakes, the wrong relationship enters the next stage."[6] The sexual sinner will begin making excuses for his or her behavior, always wanting to be with his or her lover. At this point, Mylander urged his readers to take charge of their own direction with three essential steps.[7]

1. *Fact*. The fact of our relationship to God is that our old self was crucified with Christ (see Romans 6:6 and Galatians 2:20). The Christian has been crucified and raised to new life through the indwelling of the Spirit of God within him. Therefore, we must always remind ourselves of the fact of who and what we are in Christ. No matter how we *feel* in the face of temptation, the *fact* is that we are new persons in Christ Jesus.

2. *Faith*. Faith grabs hold of God's promises and personalizes the death and resurrection of Christ into our daily walk with God. We must believe that He has set us free from sin and live like it. We can't let temptation defeat us; instead we must claim the victory by faith.

3. *Force*. Faith must be actualized or put into force by obedience. As we obey God's commands we begin to grow in our personal discipline. Romans 6:12–13 urges us not to "let sin reign in [our] mortal bodies" and not to yield our members as "instruments of unrighteousness." Commenting on this passage, Mylander stated: "With each action the Christian chooses

to make the parts of his body a force for God or a force for Satan."[8]

These three steps can help us focus on the problem of temptation, face it squarely, and defeat it soundly. As Mylander has observed, a half-hearted, double-minded, lukewarm Christian will never be able to overcome sexual temptation. He is a sitting duck for Satan's shotgun of sensuality.

If you have already given in to sexual temptation, you are in a very dangerous position. No matter what you think is good about what you are doing, God says it is wrong; therefore, He will not bless it. Persistence in sin only invites His displeasure and His judgment.

## SEXUAL MISBEHAVIOR

Sexual sins vary from adultery and premarital sex to prostitution and homosexuality. The Bible makes no attempt to categorize which wrong sexual behaviors are worse; it simply calls the wrong behavior sin. The apostle Paul called it dishonoring one's body (Romans 1:24) and clearly stated that God's will for our lives is to abstain from fornication, or sexual sin (1 Thessalonians 4:3). In his Second Letter to Timothy, Paul urged him to "flee also youthful lusts" (2 Timothy 2:22).

Deviation from the biblical norm for sex involves sex with anyone to whom one is not married. This includes premarital sex, extramarital sex (or adultery), and homosexuality (involvement with someone of the same sex). Other sexual sins include incest (sex with a close blood relative), pedophilia (sex with a child), rape (forcing sexual intercourse on another person), molestation (sexual touching of a minor), prostitution (selling one's self sexually), transvestism (sexual arousal from dressing in the clothes of the opposite sex), transsexualism (people who undergo sex-change operations or who believe they are members of the opposite sex), exhibitionism (exposing one's nakedness to others), and bestiality (sex with animals).[9]

Scripture clearly condemns virtually every one of these

sexual practices as sinful behavior.[10] Don't fall for the excuse that what you have done is so bad that it can't be forgiven. There is only one unpardonable sin in the Bible, and it is not sex![11]

Sexual sin has many possible negative consequences: guilt, bitterness, jealousy, anger, and disease. Perhaps the most feared consequence is not the spouse's discovery that he or she has been betrayed, but the individual's risk of contracting venereal disease or AIDS. The husband or wife who "plays around" can be risking their life, as well as the life of their spouse. It is estimated that over one million people will die from AIDS in America before the turn of the century.[12]

Don't be fooled by sexual temptation. Whether it attracts you by curiosity, physical desire, or the encouragement of a friend, it can devastate your mental, emotional, physical, and spiritual well-being.

## FINDING FORGIVENESS

Forgiveness is an expression of the grace of God; it is the one thing God will grant you when no one else is willing to do so. He holds no grudges and keeps short accounts when we turn to Him. Some sins are easier for us to accept forgiveness for than other ones. Sexual sins tend to be tough ones because they involve the violation of another person.

Tim Timmons likened the sins of our past to our driving a car with an oversized rear-view mirror that blocks the windshield of the future.[13] We must learn to accept God's forgiveness, seek others' forgiveness, and then forgive ourselves. Psychologist George Alan Reckers said that the greatest need in our society is for "forgiveness and the healing of moral guilt."[14]

What if you seek forgiveness and the other person won't grant it? Then your conscience is clear. David Seamands said, "The reason some people have never been able to forgive is that if they forgave, the last rug would be pulled out from under them and they would have no one to blame."[15]

Others are hung up on forgiving themselves. Let me tell you clearly that self-punishment will not atone for your sins. Jesus Christ already atoned for them on the cross. You can't pay for them because He has already paid in full. William Coleman said, "If we refuse to forget the past, we sacrifice the present and the future."[16] Lewis Smedes put it this way: "When you forgive yourself, you rewrite your script."[17]

Many people have crucified themselves between the thief of yesterday and the thief of tomorrow. As a result, they can't enjoy their freedom today. You can't go back and relive or undo the past. But with the following helps, you can change the present and thus change the future.

1. *Ask God's forgiveness*. Stop making excuses for your sin. Confess it and ask God to forgive you. The Bible promises: "If we confess our sins, He is faithful and just to forgive us our sins and to cleanse us from all unrighteousness" (1 John 1:9).

2. *Accept His forgiveness by faith*. Stop condemning yourself or thinking that you are unworthy of God's grace. We are all unworthy. That is why God gives grace: even though I don't deserve it, He offers me full pardon.

3. *Celebrate your new freedom*. The Bible promises, "There is therefore now no condemnation to those who are in Christ Jesus" (Romans 8:1). The judgment of God against your sin has been taken by Christ. The pardon has been extended by the Father and sealed to your heart by the Holy Spirit. The transaction is settled. Believe it! Celebrate it!

Charles Mylander said, "A Christian feels forgiven when he can look back on a painful memory and the stinger is gone."[18] Then, self-condemnation gives way to hope; the future looks brighter, and the path ahead more clear.

Remember, you are not alone in your journey. Many others have walked this way before you. They have learned to walk by faith, believing God's promises, receiving His grace, and accepting His forgiveness.

I will never forget the day I sat on the beach at Ft. Myers, writing my sins in the sand and watching the waves wash them away. The whole experience became a visible symbol of the reality of God's grace in my life. Perhaps it would help you to write your sins on pieces of paper, then tear them up, and watch the wind blow them away. You must *shake off the dust* and move on to a new and better life.

## Chapter 7

# Divorce:
# The Epidemic of
# Fractured Families

"JAY, YOU WILL just have to understand," my mother used to say every time things fell apart at home. But the problem was that I didn't understand. I felt hurt and betrayed. I wanted to scream out, but I couldn't.

Rejection is one of the greatest side effects of divorce. Kids feel it, spouses feel it, and even relatives feel it. Nobody believes that divorce doesn't hurt anyone. In fact, even secular writers now admit that it hurts everyone involved.[1] The tragedy is that children are the real losers. Old cliches like "kids are resilient" or "they will bounce back" just aren't true.[2]

## CHILDREN OF DIVORCE

With a national divorce rate of nearly 50 percent in the United States, it is now estimated that 30 percent of all children born in the 1980s will become the victims of parental divorce before they reach the age of eighteen. On this basis Dr. Edward Dobson said, "These statistics are forcing the church to face the reality of ministering to single-parent families and the children of divorce."[3]

Dr. Dobson further commented that divorce is a "deeply traumatic experience for children."[4] He noted that mental health experts are increasingly recognizing its bad effects in the children's feelings of rejection, loss, loneliness, hopelessness, and insecurity. Many children even blame themselves for divorce. In an attempt to manage their emotions, kids use a variety of psychological defenses, including denial, avoidance, blame, guilt, and just plain courage.[5]

I remember talking to a young teenage girl in Dallas, Texas, whose parents had recently divorced. She was angry and confused.

"It's just not fair," she said, pulling on the ends of her hair as she talked.

"How are you handling it?" I asked.

"Not very well," she replied. "I just don't believe they could do this to me."

"Well, they probably didn't mean to do it to *you*," I suggested. "They are really doing it to each other."

"But I'm the one caught in the middle," she almost screamed. "How am I supposed to choose sides or even begin to understand who's at fault?"

Tiffany was typical of many teenagers who feel angry and confused by their parents' divorces. Divorce had brought confusion and uncertainty into her life. It raised questions she did not want to have to answer, such as, Who am I going to live with? Are we going to move? Will I have to change schools? What am I going to tell my friends?

For teenagers these are tough questions. They strike at the very heart of a teen's existence and threaten his or her future.

Dobson listed six negative effects divorce has on children:[6]

1. *Anger*. Recent opinion surveys show that almost all young people experience anger at one or both parents when a divorce occurs.

2. *Fear*. Many kids fear being forgotten or abandoned by divorcing parents. Others fear the future, which seems bleak and unstable.

3. *Loss of identity*. Since the self-image of children is closely related to family structure and development, children of divorce feel a great sense of insecurity and personal loss.

4. *Loneliness*. Wallerstein and Kelly observed that the

children of divorce feel lonely and isolated. They are often "paralyzed by their own conflicting loyalties . . . [thus] many children refrained from choice and felt alone and desolate, with no place to turn for comfort or parenting."[7]

5. *School Performance.* Nearly half of all the children of divorce experience an immediate and noticeable decline in school performance. They seem preoccupied with the conflicts of their parents and the effect of those conflicts on them.

6. *Parent-Child Relationships.* While the effects of divorce on the parent-child relationship vary within given families, it has become increasingly clear that many children take sides and reject one or both parents as being bad. In most cases the one parent influences the child to believe that he or she is right and the other parent is wrong.

At least half of the children studied showed signs of anger, pain, and hostility, long after the divorce. In most cases this surfaced as depression and low self-esteem.

Researchers Swihart and Brigham isolated several key factors presented in the following chart that lessen or increase the impact of divorce:[8]

### Divorce Adjustment Factors

| Lessens Impact | Increases Impact of Divorce |
|---|---|
| 1. Parents do not put children in the middle. | 1. Children are asked to choose between parents. |
| 2. Children are told about the separation. | 2. Children are not told about separation or are given little information. |
| 3. Children are aware of the conflict between parents. | 3. Parents hide conflict and angry feelings. |
| 4. Children are not held responsible for the divorce. | 4. Children are made to feel that divorce is their fault. |
| 5. Children are not used for parental support. | 5. Parent relies on child for personal support. |
| 6. Children receive support from significant people. | 6. Children are isolated from family friends. |

| | |
|---|---|
| 7. Parents resolve personal anger. | 7. Parents are unable to resolve anger. |
| 8. The absent parent stays in contact with the child. | 8. The absent parent has little contact with child. |
| 9. Siblings. | 9. Only child. |
| 10. Family moves into a new schedule fairly quickly. | 10. Family remains disorganized long after separation. |
| 11. Other environmental factors remain stable. | 11. Life is greatly changed: school, neighborhood, parent's work hours and so on. |
| 12. Each parent frequently spends individual time with each child. | 12. Little individual attention is given to children. |
| 13. Parents assist each child with individual adjustment reaction. | 13. Parents are not aware of individual adjustment reactions. |
| 14. Children are allowed to grieve. | 14. Loss is denied—no grieving is allowed. |
| 15. Family focuses on the positive and the future. | 15. Family focuses on present calamity. |
| 16. Parents had previous good relationship with child. | 16. Child had not previously felt loved or valued by parents. |

In discussing what could be done about the effects of divorce on children, Dobson urged that parents consider the impact their separation or divorce could have upon their children.[9] He noted that parents who are caught in the conflict of divorce become so consumed with their own problems that they often give little attention the needs of their children.

In his book *The Total Family,* Dr. Ed Hindson recommended the following to parents who are suffering the trauma of divorce:[10]

1. *Don't blame God for your circumstances.*

2. *Don't criticize your divorced partner in front of your children* (remember, he or she is still their parent).

3. *Don't condemn yourself for circumstances beyond your control:* "I wish I had done better"; "If I had said this, maybe he wouldn't have left."

4. *Don't wish you were someone else* (that is irresponsibly avoiding reality). Such day-dreaming will ruin your kids.

5. *Don't speculate endlessly about what might have been if.* . . . The time has come to fully accept things as they are. If your partner has left and remarried, the scripture advises not to take him back (see Deuteronomy 24:1–4).

6. *Don't over-"spiritualize" your problems.* Your kids will see right through all that drippy talk about how you are really satisfied that things worked out the way they did. Don't misquote Romans 8:28.

7. *Don't excuse yourself either.* It takes two to tangle. Don't put all the blame on your partner.

8. *Don't become overly dependent on the wrong people.* Stay away from married men/women. Don't constantly run to your friends with your problems; it will confuse you. Learn to place your greatest dependence on the Lord Himself.

9. *Don't dominate your kids* (so they won't turn out like you). You may drive them off by being too much of a martyr.

10. *Don't worry about the future; trust God.*

## DIVORCE AND THE CHURCH

Diane and I recently counseled with a wife in Texas who related the story of her impending divorce.

"I've been married twenty years. I'm thirty-eight years old, have two children, and I am out of work," she began.

"How long have you been separated from your husband?" Diane asked her.

"Almost a year now," she replied. "In fact, the divorce will be final next week." Then she began to cry softly, and her hands began to shake. "I don't want a divorce," she insisted, "but I can't stop it."

"How did this all get started?" I asked.

"My husband and I just started arguing one day and he said, 'I've had enough,' and walked out," she replied. "I thought he would come back, but he didn't. Another couple took him in for a while. But it wasn't long until he met another woman and moved in with her." Then she said something I will never forget.

"Jay," she pleaded, "my husband is a Christian. He knows better. What has gone wrong with us?"

Her question is one that the church universal needs to face, because divorce today is as serious a problem *in* the church as it is *outside* the church. One divorced couple provided this observation:

> Less than a generation ago, married people knew little about the world of the formerly married; it was a semisecret society. Its members were close-mouthed about their feelings and experiences because, in the larger society, divorce was still considered a tragedy and, in many quarters, something of a disgrace. . . . But in recent years, divorce has become so common, so much more approved, so widely discussed.[11]

The cumulative impact of divorced people, claiming they have found relief, freedom, and sexual excitement, has dented the ranks of Christian couples. That impact reaches us through television, videos, movies, books, magazines, and personal encounters. Forgetting what the scriptures say about the sanctity and permanence of marriage, we have run headlong after the world, uncritically accepting its philosophies. I hear it all the time in my encounters with people.

"But Jay, I just don't love her any more," one pastor told me of his wife. "We just don't get along, and it's hurting the kids," his wife replied. "We may just as well hang it up," they agreed.

Ours is a society long on pleasure and short on commitment. We want whatever makes us feel good, even if it hurts someone else. Jesus said that people get divorced because of the hardness of their hearts (Matthew 19:8). Given our rate of divorce, our society must have a lot of hard-hearted, selfish people. I know that sounds harsh, but I know what divorce can do to people. I have seen its awful effects firsthand more often than I care to remember.

Whenever you choose to divorce, you are taking a chance that your children will not recover. Sometimes they are scarred for life. "I just can't believe my parents could love me and do this," one teenager told me about his parents' divorce.

The consequences of divorce on the partner who wants to keep the marriage together are also devastating. "I would wake up with attacks of uncontrollable chills," a forty-year-old woman in Indianapolis said. "I had nightmares about jagged cliffs and rushing rivers."

"For me, my only thought was how to get from one day to the next without cracking up," said a thirty-two-year-old woman in Denver.

"I felt physically and emotionally broken," said a forty-three-year-old man in Little Rock. "I couldn't sleep and had nightmares all night. When morning came, I didn't want to get up and face another day."

A man in Mobile told me, "I just got drunk and stayed drunk, so I wouldn't have to think about it."

Divorce, for many, is a nightmare from which they cannot wake up. Although I do not intend to condemn those whose marriages have already failed, I want to appeal to you who are struggling with your current marriage not to give up. You can learn to forgive each other, reconcile your differences, and love again. In fact, love is the most natural emotion in the world. All you have to do to set it free is to stop hating each other.

After one of our crusades in Memphis, a young couple sat down on the steps of the church platform and asked to talk to me.

"We were going to go to court tomorrow to finalize our divorce," they said. "But we decided to come here tonight to hear you just in case there was any hope."

I had preached that night on the love of God and shared part of my life story. They were obviously attracted to what I had said.

"Do you believe that God really loves you?" I asked them.

"Yes, we do."

"Have you ever committed your lives to Him?"

Their heads dropped as they admitted that they had. "We have come to church here for years," they said, and then added, "I guess we know all the right answers."

"If God lives within you and He is love, then the only reason you can't love each other is because you won't let Him take control," I suggested.

We had talked for about twenty minutes, when Glenn, the husband, said, "I want to love Judy, but I can see now that I really haven't tried."

"I guess I haven't either," said Judy.

I suggested that we pray together and that they ask God's forgiveness and one another's forgiveness. As we prayed together, Glenn's tears began rolling off his cheeks onto their clasped hands. At first Judy smiled appreciatively, and then she began to cry as well.

God was healing the hurts of their souls and He was putting their marriage back together. I don't care what has gone wrong in the past, God can forgive it and heal it and redirect your lives in the future. Stop denying Him the opportunity to work. Turn to him with faith and hope. He will not reject you. In fact, He stands ready with open arms to receive you and fill you with His love.

## STARTING OVER

Betty was an attractive blonde in her early forties when I first met her in Orlando during one of our crusades. She had two teenagers who had heard me in a school assembly and had invited her to attend our evening rally. As we talked together after the rally, she related that her husband had left her two years earlier.

"The divorce was final a year ago," she said. "I didn't want it and I've been crying ever since. I'm concerned about my children, but I haven't handled my own problems very well. Can God forgive me and give me a new life?"

"Of course He can!" I assured her. "You can't spend the rest of your life blaming yourself for what went wrong."

As we talked together, she related how she had tried to condemn her husband to their children. "It has them divided and confused," she said. "I realize now this is wrong and it is only hurting the kids worse."

"Are you willing to put it behind you?" I asked her. Then I explained the concept of *shaking off the dust* of one's past and moving on with the rest of one's life.

She smiled. "That's what I need."

We prayed together and she committed her life to Christ, asking Him to forgive and cleanse her and to set her free from the bondage of the past. When we finished, her face was beaming radiantly. As she ran to tell her children what she had done, I could see the joy in all of them. She has worked hard at establishing a beautiful Christian home which God has blessed abundantly.

For many divorcees, starting over is not an easy process. John Splinter, a singles minister in St. Louis, described the pitfalls that confront the newly divorced:[12]

1. *Denial.* The initial reaction of divorcing couples is to refuse to believe they are being divorced. Their denial takes the form of "This is not happening to me" or "He/she can't do this to me" or "I'll fight this. . . . He/she will never get away with this."

2. *Alcohol or Drugs.* Some turn to artificial support from alcohol or drugs to soothe their grief during a divorce. This often leads to self-destructive behavior.

3. *Self-pity.* One spouse can use self-pity to induce guilt in the divorcing partner (and thereby gain hope of reconciliation). Or a spouse may exhibit self-pity to friends and relatives who are expected to believe "I am right; he/she is wrong."

4. *Bitterness.* Some people become inwardly bitter, whereas others turn their bitterness outward to social infighting. They get friends to take sides, spy on, pressure, or hassle the ex-spouse. Remember, bitterness cripples only *you;* it has virtually no effect on the object of your bitterness.

5. *Leaping into Another Relationship.* Newly divorced people are especially vulnerable to promiscuous sex or new re-

lationships to ease their pain, reassure their deflated egos, and send a "message" back to their former spouse. Such relationships are products of the "I don't need you, I've got someone else" mentality.

Splinter observed that all these approaches are dead ends for the divorced because they keep them from accepting the divorce, learning from it, and successfully rebuilding their lives. He warns against the dangers of self-pity, self-indulgence, dating again, and fears of remarriage.

Divorced people must accept their single status before they can properly establish a new and lasting relationship with someone else. Be patient when considering remarriage. While you are hurting, your thoughts and emotions will be clouded. Make sure you seek the advice of a pastor or counselor before you remarry. Talk the decision through with your children, parents, or other family members. Don't expect someone else to heal all your hurts. They, too, may be bringing a good deal of hurt into the relationship. Second marriages often fail because one partner puts too many emotional demands on the other.[13]

## THE FAMILY OF THE FUTURE

Projections of family life in the next century and the next millennium are anything but hopeful. One theorist, Lonnie Barbach, predicted, "The structure of families will change and the reasons for being in relationship in the future will differ from those of the past."[14] She predicted that the number of unmarried couples living together will increase and that those who do marry will do so with the foreknowledge that they are likely to divorce and remarry two or three times during their lives. Barbach noted that "divorce will be one of the societal norms."[15]

We in the Christian community must wake up to the fact that we are drifting downstream with the rest of the world. Society is disintegrating. It is coming apart at the seams, and if we don't do something to stop it, these predictions will become reality. We can't keep breaking up the home and expect our society to be stable. If you can still salvage your marriage, do it. If you are already divorced and remarried, save that marriage.

Barbara was twenty-eight years old, divorced, and remarried to a man named Tom. She had been married to Tom for two years when I first met her at our crusade.

"Did I do the right thing?" she asked, "or should I go back to my first husband?"

"Two wrongs don't make a right," I told her. "Besides, the Bible (Deuteronomy 24:1–4) forbids you to divorce your second husband and remarry the first one."

"I thought I had found the right guy this time," she sighed, quickly adding, "Now, I'm not sure."

"You can't spend the rest of your life second-guessing yourself," I said. "You've got to determine to make it work this time."

Many couples do not make it because they are unwilling to try. You have to be willing to pay the price of commitment. Don't let a divorced friend convince you that divorced people are happier. They are not, and all the psychological studies ever done on divorced people have proved that. Divorce may provide an artificial sense of freedom and excitement at first, but that eventually fades as reality sets in.[16]

Although divorce is painful, it doesn't have to keep hurting. It is no different from any other loss we experience in life. It only hurts as much as we let it hurt. Now, I'm not suggesting that you artificially dismiss the pain. But I am saying that you need to deal with the pain in the light of God's grace. He knows all about your life and its failures. He knows you better than anyone knows you, including yourself. In fact, if you really want to understand yourself, you need to see yourself as He sees you.

First, God sees you as a sinner. He knows that you are basically selfish and self-centered. He can see right through all your excuses and alibis. He knows what really makes you tick. But despite this, He loves you like no one ever could love you.

Before you can properly love yourself enough to forgive yourself, you have to be convinced that He loves you. Before you can ever learn to love someone again, you have to be convinced that He can love them through you.

Love is not something to fear because you feel incapable of expressing it. Rather, it is the gift of God, the fruit of His Spirit who lives within each believer. We can love others because He loved us. We can also love them because He who lives within us loves them through us. This is one of the great principles of the new life we have in Christ.

Our ability to love and forgive those who hurt us in life is the key to freeing our conscience from the guilt of bitterness of the past. If your parents hurt you by divorcing, don't keep on hating them. Forgive them, love them, reach out to them. They need your love as much as you need theirs.

For many years I could not understand why my parents divorced. I blamed them for not loving me or caring enough to stay together for my sake. It was not until I was an adult that I began to understand what had gone wrong. Then I could see the regret in their faces. But their regret was futile because they could not go back and undo what they had done.

As the years went by, my father came to the end of himself. Alcohol ruined his life, destroyed our home, and nearly killed him. But through the help of professionals, he was able to quit drinking and get his life together. Today, he is helping other alcoholics and problem drinkers.

My mother also had a turning-point experience and discovered what God's love was really all about. Although they never remarried, both of my parents came to see the harm their divorce had caused and they did everything they could to correct it.

I will never forget a man I'll call Bill, who came forward for prayer in one of our crusades in Nashville. Once a pastor, Bill had divorced his wife and run off with another woman. He sobbed uncontrollably as he started down the aisle. I immediately came off the platform to embrace him.

"Oh, Jay, please forgive me," he sobbed as he wept on my shoulder.

"Of course I will forgive you, Bill," I said. "But God has already forgiven you."

"I can't undo the wrong I've done," he said, trying to fight back the tears.

"You don't have to, man," I said. "Jesus already took care of that on the cross."

"But I feel so unworthy."

"We are all unworthy, remember? That is why we need His grace."

"Can I ever serve God again?" Bill asked sincerely.

"Of course, you can," I replied, "but you have to shake off all this guilt and find direction for your life. No one is stopping you from serving God, but you."

As we prayed together that night, I knew it would be a tough road, but I knew God would use him again, and He has.

Most of us want a quick fix for our mistakes, but there aren't any. We have to be willing to face the consequences of our sin and still be willing to move beyond it to a life of service and fruitfulness for God.

You may feel that your divorce is the end, but I want to tell you it is not. The grace of God is greater than all of our failures and mistakes. Stop running away from God and run back into His arms of love. Like the father waiting for his prodigal son, God is waiting for you to come home to Him.

# Chapter 8 ◀

# Child Abuse: Violence in the Family

IT WAS A hot summer night in Ft. Worth, Texas. I had been conducting a crusade for nearly a week when Gail, a social worker, brought Jenny to me. Jenny was a black-haired, nine-year-old girl with small scars on her face and arms. As Gail and I talked, Jenny looked down at the floor and dragged her foot on the carpet.

"Do you see these?" Gail asked pointing to the scars on Jenny's face. "These are cigarette burns!" she said, with terror in her eyes.

"How did this happen?" I asked.

Gail had been assigned to Jenny's case a week earlier. She explained that Jenny's mother had used cigarettes to punish the child whenever she felt she was misbehaving.

"Her case goes to court in two months," Gail said. "I know there isn't much you can do for her now, but I wanted to know how often this kind of thing goes on. Most of these kids have a very low self-image, are poor students, and don't have much of a future."

"How could her mother do this?" I asked.

"She was an abused child herself when she was growing up," Gail said. "She got pregnant at fifteen and was a mother by the time she was sixteen. She just couldn't handle the responsibility. Because she had been roughed up as a kid, that was the only way she knew how to deal with children."

Then Gail looked at me and said something I will never forget. "Jay, you speak to a lot of kids; please warn them against this sort of thing. Many of them will get pregnant and become young mothers and could easily turn out the same way."

As we talked, I remembered some of the unpleasant experiences of my childhood—the hurt and the embarrassment. And I recalled thinking, *I'm not ever going to tell anyone what happened.*

## FAMILY VIOLENCE

Child abuse is a major problem in America. In a nation that has so much material wealth, we seem to have so little spiritually. Family violence is steadily increasing. One home in six is the scene of husbands' and wives' striking each other. Three out of five homes are racked with the violence of parents against children or children against each other.[1]

Approximately two million women and children are battered and beaten by family members every year. Police records demonstrate the use of extensive and often lethal forms of violence by parents. Children have been beaten, mutilated, castrated, burned, and killed by violent parents. It is estimated that more American children under the age of five die from parentally inflicted injuries than from tuberculosis, whooping cough, polio, measles, diabetes, rheumatic fever, and appendicitis combined.[2]

Estimates vary on child deaths inflicted by family members, but a reasonable estimate is 5,000 per year (U.S. Senate 1983). (Most family violence leading to murder involves adults.) In New York City alone, in 1979, more people died from intrafamilial homicide than have been killed in acts of violence in Northern Ireland or South Africa combined.[3]

In Atlanta, 31 percent of all homicides are the result of domestic quarrels.[4] In Detroit, 52 percent of all aggravated assaults reported to the police are between husbands and wives.[5] One legal researcher estimated that the police answer more calls involving family conflicts than all the calls for criminal incidents combined—including murders, rapes, robberies, assaults, and muggings combined. In fact, more police officers die answering family disturbance calls than die because of any other single crime.[6]

A 1975 nationwide study revealed that 13 percent of all parents have struck their child with an object other than would be used in a normal spanking; 5 percent have thrown an object at their child; 3 percent have bit, kicked, or punched their child; 1 percent have admitted beating up their child at least once in the previous year; and 3 percent have threatened their child with a gun or knife during their lifetime. One child in 1,000 was actually shot or stabbed by his parents during the year of the study.[7]

Ironically, this study also revealed that *mothers* were more likely to use violence against a child than fathers were. Perhaps this can be explained by the fact that mothers generally spend more time with children than fathers do. Another possibility is that children tend to interfere with mothers' plans more than fathers' plans. One Boston housewife described it like this:

> I can feel it coming more or less; I think it's depression or frustration. I get so fed up with the house and knowing I've gotta watch the kids . . . feed them . . . do the dishes. Like you get up in the morning, you cook breakfast, you do dishes, you clean the house. Next thing you know, it's lunch time. While you're fixing lunch, they're out there messing up two or three rooms. . . . That's when it happens—Boom![8]

## WHAT GOES WRONG?

Several factors contribute to child abuse. Researchers who have studied this issue in depth have found that children who were abused often grow up to be abusive parents.[9] Research on murderers and assassins has showed that they all had violent childhood experiences. In his diary, Arthur Bremer, George Wallace's would-be assassin wrote: "My mother must have thought I was a canoe, she paddled me so much."[10] Lee Harvey Oswald, Sirhan Sirhan, and Charles Manson all experienced violent childhoods.

Psychologist Ralph Welsh claimed that he has never examined a violent juvenile delinquent who did not come from an extremely violent background.[11] Although violence at school, work, play, or even on television may contribute to our violent society, violence in our homes is a far more serious source of child abuse.

In a national survey on child abuse, the following factors were determined to be predictable indicators of potential child abuse:[12]

Abuse by Either Parent
1. Verbal aggression against child.
2. Conflict between husband and wife.
3. Physical violence between husband and wife.

Abuse by Mothers
1. Husband was verbally abusive to wife.
2. Husband was a manual laborer.
3. Husband dissatisfied with standard of living.
4. Wife was a manual worker.
5. Wife was thirty or under.
6. Wife was punished physically by her father.

Abuse by Fathers
1. Two or more children at home.
2. Married less than ten years.
3. Wife is a full-time housewife.
4. Lived in neighborhood less than two years.
5. No participation in organized groups.
6. Grew up in family where mother hit father.
7. Husband was physically punished by his mother.

In another study conducted by the Welfare Administration and Brandeis University, it was discovered that the following factors generally contributed to child abuse:[13]

1. Psychological rejection.
2. Disciplinary measures taken in uncontrolled anger.
3. Male babysitters taking out sadistic and sexual impulses on children.
4. Mentally or emotionally disturbed parents/caretakers.
5. Quarrels between parents under the influence of alcohol.

Overloaded with stress and pressure, many parents tragically have no spiritual resources to rely on for strength. They get upset and blow up at their children. When this occurs frequently, it drives the child away from his or her parents and causes rebellion against their authority.

## MY MOTHER NEVER STOPPED IT

Donna was a sixteen-year-old junior at a large high school in Florida. She was president of her class and very involved in school activities. After one of my assemblies, she came up to me and said: "I don't believe in God. In fact, I don't believe in anyone but me."

"You must have had some people hurt you or let you down to say that," I replied.

"How would you know?" she asked sarcastically.

"I had some people hurt me; that's how," I said.

Her expression changed. She became more pensive and serious. "Were you ever abused?" she asked.

"Yes, I was," I replied. "It's a terrible experience for anyone."

"I don't want to talk about it here," she said.

"That's fine," I replied. "Why don't you come to our crusade service tonight, and my wife and I will talk to you about it afterward."

That night it was raining hard as the service began, and I wondered if Donna would make the effort to be there. During the song service I spotted her coming down the aisle looking for a seat. She was soaking wet but didn't seem to mind. Before long she was caught up in the service and what was happening on the platform.

Several teenagers shared their testimonies of faith in Christ. Some told of their personal battles with drugs or alcohol. Then Barbara, a girl from a neighboring high school, stepped up to the mike and hesitantly said that something terrible had happened to her when she was younger that made her very bitter against God and her parents. "I'd rather not go into it," she said. "But it nearly ruined my life." She then told how she had committed her life to Christ and had come to forgive those who hurt her.

As I glanced toward Donna, I could see the empathy on her face. As Barbara talked further, Donna began to get a look of hope and expectation.

During the invitation, Donna came forward to give her life to Christ. She stood quietly at the altar as I explained how to receive Christ as one's own personal Savior. She was one of about two hundred people who bowed their heads with me that night to commit themselves to Christ. Then to my surprise, Barbara went and stood next to Donna and offered to go with her to the counseling room.

Diane and I waited until Donna came out of the counseling room. She was smiling brightly and walking briskly as she came toward us.

"Well, I did it," she announced. "I just gave my life to Christ and I feel great."

Then she explained that she had opened up to Barbara about the terrible physical abuse she had received at home when she was younger. In turn, Barbara had shared her experiences with Donna. As we all talked together, I began to emphasize the need for honesty in dealing with this situation.

"You can't let this keep happening," Diane told her.

"It hasn't now for a long time," Donna reassured us. "It

was mostly when I was younger. My mother knew about it, but she never tried to stop it."

She described a terrible stepfather who beat her severely with a belt and tied her to a bed rail with it for hours at a time.

"How long did this go on?" I asked.

"Several years," she replied, "until he and my mother divorced."

"Have you and your mom ever talked about it?" Diane asked.

"Not for a long time," Donna said. "I guess I'm still pretty angry and bitter toward her for letting it happen."

"Don't you think you ought to forgive her and ask her to forgive you?" Diane suggested.

"I know I'll never feel right until I do," Donna said.

As we talked further, we agreed to have the local pastor go with Donna to tell her mother about the bitterness she was holding inside her and to ask her forgiveness. Later, when they did go, her mother broke down sobbing, asking Donna to forgive her for failing her as a mother. After many tears, they were truly reconciled to one another.

Physical abuse is a serious matter that needs to be reported to the proper authorities for the child's protection. But in this case the abuser was gone from the home, leaving the mother and daughter with the ugly memory of what had happened.

In time, Donna's mother also gave her life to the Lord and became a dynamic witness for Christ. Together, they began to rebuild their lives around a positive relationship. The old hurts and bitternesses were gone. There was a joy and happiness in their lives like they had never known. The emotional healing of God's grace was at work, and it was marvelous to behold.

## EVERYONE IS AFRAID OF MY DAD

Only a few weeks later, I met Brian. He was a ninth grader. His father had brutally abused him most of his life. He had a collection of broken bones, bruises, and even cuts from their encounters.

"It's pretty bad, even now," he said.

"Why don't you go to the police or the state welfare authorities?" I asked.

"He's pretty influential on this side of town," Brian said. "His relatives would fix it so he would get off."

"Have you ever told your mother how you feel?" I asked, looking right at him.

"She knows," he replied bluntly.

"Does she ever try to stop him?" I asked.

"Not really," he said. "She's afraid of him too."

"It sounds to me like you are going to have to confront the situation or it's not going to change," I suggested.

"How can I?"

"Well, for starters we need to ask the principal for advice. He will know what to do."

Reluctantly, Brian accompanied me to the principal's office. Together we helped him see that nothing short of a proper reporting of the abuse would ever make his father stop. The principal knew of a crisis intervention home for physically abused kids and recommended that we take Brian there for help and protection.

Although the action that followed was not pleasant, it helped greatly. Brian fully disclosed the nature of what had been happening to him, and his father was confronted by the authorities. After appropriate legal action and counseling, the entire family was able to resolve the conflict. Today, they are all back together and doing very well.

## ABUSERS NEED HELP TOO

W. C. Fields once said, "Any man who hates children and dogs cannot be all bad."[14] Although this may have been said in jest, it reflects an inherent attitude of many in our society. Unfortunately, this dislike reaches the level of hatred in many cases and leads to the death, maiming, or psychological damage of thousands of kids every year.

I clearly remember my own feelings the first time I counseled a child abuser. He was a twenty-eight year old named Andy. He was living with his wife and infant son near the church I was pastoring. Neighbors had become concerned about the screaming child and wondered what was happening. They finally convinced the wife to talk to her family physician, who was a member of our church. He in turn asked me to sit in on the counseling process.

As she began talking, she unloaded the agony of her soul. She had been working as a salesperson at a local mall while her husband, who worked nights, kept the baby during the day. She had noticed several bruises on the baby, but believed the explanations given by her husband. On one occasion the baby's arm was actually broken. The father claimed that the baby had fallen, but the mother began to doubt his explanation.

When she confronted him, Andy admitted his striking the baby violently in order to get him to stop crying. He promised to stop any further outbursts of anger and made her promise not to tell anyone. But he didn't stop. Eventually, however, through the pleading of her neighbors, she went to her family physician for help.

As we talked with Andy, I became angry and resentful. I wondered how he could do such a thing. But I began to realize that he, too, was in need of help. He had been racked with guilt and emotional anguish. The entire incident had threatened his marriage, his job, and his future.

During our first session in the doctor's office, he began to sob uncontrollably. "I'm so terrible," he said repeatedly.

"What you have done is terrible," the doctor said wisely, "but you don't have to keep on being terrible."

"Do you think you can help me?"

"Yes," said the doctor. "First, I want you to submit to psychiatric evaluation and treatment to get at the root of this. And secondly, I want you to counsel with this pastor to see if he can help you spiritually."

Andy agreed and we set the process in motion. In the next months he came to realize his inability to handle stress on his job and his unwillingness to communicate with his wife. He also saw his need for forgiveness, and as a result, he gave his life to Christ. As we all worked together, Andy and his wife began to see that there was hope for reconciliation and healing in their relationship.

In the months that followed Andy's conversion to Christ, he became a changed person. He responded positively to counseling and was eventually reunited with his wife and son. Today they have three children and are actively involved in a church in their community. Andy's counselor told him he had been pleasantly surprised by the change that had come over Andy.

"So was I," Andy responded. "It was God at work in my soul. I had nothing to do with it. I just surrendered to Him and let Him take control."

## WHAT ABOUT CHILD DISCIPLINE?

"I don't believe in discipline," a young mother once told me. "These people who spank their kids are all child abusers!"

"I totally disagree with you," I told her. "I'm convinced that people who abuse children through physical violence often do so because they don't have a philosophy of child discipline. They just let their kids run wild until they do something that upsets them and then they explode."

"Why do you say that?"

"Because every child abuser I have ever talked to admitted he or she did not have a plan of discipline for their children."

The Bible says, "He who troubles his own house will inherit the wind" (Proverbs 11:29). God holds parents responsible for the spiritual development of their children (see Ephesians 6:1–4). Therefore, the Bible is filled with advice about rearing children. It makes it clear that the key to effective child rearing is the parent. You and I must set the standards of behavior for our home and follow through with discipline that is aimed at correction, not just punishment.

The Bible says: "Foolishness is bound up in the heart of a child, but the rod of correction will drive it far from him" (Proverbs 22:15). But scripture also warns parents not to "provoke [your] children to wrath" (Ephesians 6:4).

The proper balance must always exist between love and discipline. Overbalanced parents tend to become too permissive or overly authoritarian. Scripture urges us to keep both in a proper balance, while helping our children develop a strong and positive self-image. Christian psychologist Dr. James Dobson stated:

> Respectful and responsible children result from families where the proper combination of *love* and *discipline* is present. Both of these ingredients must be applied in necessary quantities. An absence of either is often disastrous.[15]

Let me suggest the following steps for effective child discipline as a preventative for child abuse.

1. *Instruction.* Parents need to teach their children right from wrong, providing a moral standard for behavior in the home. Too many parents never teach their children what they expect of them and leave their children confused about their behavior. Set standards and guidelines based upon biblical principles.

2. *Communication.* Learn to talk to your kids openly and honestly. Listen to them just as openly. Fear of reprisal will inhibit your kids from freely talking with you. Children tend to tell parents what they want to hear. If you really want to know what is going on in your children's lives, let them talk about it.

3. *Confrontation.* Don't be afraid to confront wrong behavior, but do it lovingly as well as firmly. Kids need to know that their parents are in charge. Otherwise, they will try to take over by default. Don't be afraid to reprimand or to spank them when they need it, but do so with caution and restraint. Never spank out of anger and frustration.

4. *Reassurance.* After using discipline, make sure you give your children the reassurance of your love. Make sure they un-

derstand your discipline is not an act of rejection, but one of genuine concern for their well-being.

One of the easiest mistakes to make in a disciplinary situation is to allow your personal pride to be involved. Look beyond the fact that the child has defied your authority, and instead, focus on teaching the child how to respond the next time and why he should respond that way. I tell my children that the reason I want them to respond at my first request is so they can learn to respond to God at His first request. I tell them He may not repeat that same instruction to them, and as a result, they will miss out on a blessing in God's plan for their life.

Another mistake we make is to answer "Because I said so!" This is the easiest response and takes no energy on our part, but it doesn't instruct the child. I try to show my child from scripture what God says and that I am following His instructions as a parent. My ultimate goal is to teach them to follow the instruction of God in scripture. Discipline is literally to "make a disciple" or "make a learner."

Another important step is to restore the relationship. Parents do have hurt feelings when rejected by a child. A child needs to learn how to ask for forgiveness and how to be forgiven. We also need to pray together in a time of confession to and repentance before God.

All of this may seem like a lot of trouble—and it is! But it carries preventive measures for the years ahead. Remember that discipline is a time of instruction, not of punishment. Punishment carries with it anger. Discipline is always born out of love. The external discipline you carefully administer today will produce internal discipline for tomorrow.

Dr. James Dobson suggested five key factors in parental discipline of children.[16]

1. Encourage and develop their respect for you as parents. This is a critical factor in child management.

2. Communicate with the child. Some of the best opportunities often occur after times of discipline.

   3. Control without nagging.
   4. Don't saturate the child with excessive materialism.
   5. Avoid extremes in control and love.

Dobson's points further confirm the parents' need to balance love and discipline. This balance leads to a healthy self-image in children.

In another of his books, *Hide or Seek,* Dr. Dobson discusses the issue of building self-esteem in your child:

> Loving your child, therefore, is only half of the task of
> building self-esteem. The element of respect must be
> added if you are to counterbalance the insults which
> society will later throw at him. Unless *somebody*
> believes in his worth, the world can be a cold and
> lonely place, indeed.[17]

Parents are the most influential persons in a child's life. Long before adolescent peer pressure sets in, we have ten or more years to build positive character qualities into the lives of our children. We must get started early if we want to raise positive and productive teenagers. A teen's mental and emotional well-being depends upon his relationship to God and his parents.

Never underestimate the vital and important role you play in your child's life. You are shaping his or her future every day. Your attitudes about the basic issues of life are influencing your child's attitudes about those same issues. That is why recent studies have revealed that parents' attitudes are even more important than those of a child's peers in formulating his or her basic philosophy of life.[18]

The future of America depends on the next generation. If we parents fail them, we have little to hope for ourselves. When we are too old to do so, they must carry on the principles that alone can keep us strong and free. That cannot happen when we alienate and confuse them by our own wrong behavior. As terrible as physical abuse is, it is no more wrong than the spiritual and moral abuse rampant among today's parents. We cannot expect our children to follow an example that we ourselves are unwilling to set.

I want to urge every parent who reads this book to recommit himself to being a better parent and a better example. Whatever may have gone wrong in the past can be made right in the future if we are willing to turn things around now.

# Chapter 9

# Incest:
# Sex in
# the Family

THE BELL WAS ringing loudly as we walked down the hallway at a high school in Tampa. Kids poured out of their classrooms like a mass of humanity headed toward the gym. In a few minutes I would be speaking in an assembly program.

"It's good to have you here, Jay," the principal said as we walked along. "Its been a long time since we've had something like this. I hope you can really help these kids."

As we continued walking, I noticed a tall girl with long, dark brown hair staring at me.

"Who's that girl?" I asked the principal.

"Lisa—she's one of our best students," he replied.

She seemed to have a questioning and distant stare in her eyes, as though she were asking herself if I could be trusted.

After the assembly, she came up to me and asked if I had ever talked to someone with sexual problems other than "boy-girl stuff."

"Yes, at times," I said.

"I can't talk now," she said, "I've got to go to class. I'll come to hear you tonight. Maybe we can talk then."

That night she did not show up at the crusade service, and I assumed I would not see her again. After the service, the pastor and I decided to get something to eat at a nearby restaurant.

"Your waitress will be right with you," said the hostess as we were seated.

Looking up from the menus, we were greeted by a familiar face asking, "Can I take your order?" It was Lisa, the girl I had met earlier that day.

"I thought you were going to come to our service tonight," I said.

"I was," she replied, "but I had to work. I'll come tomorrow."

"Good enough," I said. "I'll be looking for you."

"Great," she replied, "I still want to have that talk."

The next night the place was packed and I wondered if Lisa would even get in the building. But after the service she came up to Diane and me and asked to talk, just as she had promised.

"Can we go some place private?" she asked.

"Sure, let's use the pastor's study," I suggested.

As we sat down to talk, Lisa seemed hesitant. After a few false starts, she said, "I may as well tell you the whole thing."

She began telling us about being sexually assaulted by her father during the past eight years. It was traumatic for her even to talk about it.

"I feel like I'm betraying my family," she said, "but I've got to tell someone."

She began to tell us of having sexual relations with her father since she was eleven. At times her voice reflected anger and at other times it reflected guilt, as though it were all her fault.

"I've tried to stop, but he won't take 'no' for an answer," she said desperately.

"Does your mother know about this?" Diane asked.

"I don't know," Lisa replied, "but I don't see how she could not tell something is wrong. When I was younger I asked her to tell my father to stop touching me and holding me all the time. She just said that fathers were like that and not to worry about it. Later, I could hear them arguing down the hall, but she never said any more to me about it."

Lisa was typical of thousands of teenage girls who have been sexually exploited by their fathers through incestuous relationships. Although I believe it has long been a problem, incest was once a topic nobody talked about openly. But today I hear it discussed everywhere I go.

## WHAT IS INCEST?

Incest is the practice of sexual intimacy among relatives or family members. It may be either heterosexual or homosexual in its expression and often involves stepfamily members. It may involve fathers–daughters, fathers–sons, mothers–sons, grandfathers–granddaughters, brothers–sisters, uncles–nieces, aunts–nephews, or very rarely, mothers–daughters. It is not a pleasant topic to discuss, but it is a reality in hundreds of thousands of American homes.

Teenagers are especially vulnerable to incest. As they grow up and mature sexually, almost overnight, they are often unsure of themselves sexually. In their minds they think of themselves as children. But socially they want to appear as adults. When parents or older relatives make sexual advances toward them, they tend to assume the role of obedient children, acting in compliance with their elder's demands.

Once sexual stimulation or intercourse has been reached, the children feel guilty. They cannot meet the demands for love and intimacy that are required and the secretiveness makes them feel ashamed of what they have done.[1]

Defining incest is difficult since it often involves stepfathers who are not blood relatives. Therefore, many professional counselors use the classification of "sexual activity involving genital contact between people too closely related to marry."[2] It may be related to sexual abuse, but not limited to it. Abuse generally carries the connotation of forced action or rape, whereas incest may involve only emotional intimacy with limited physical contact.

In most cases incest begins with emotional intimacy and becomes more pronounced by physical contact, exhibitionism, genital manipulation, or mutual masturbation. The trauma inflicted on the child is not limited to sexual intercourse, but to the feeling that one is not safe around the potential molester. A considerable number of child sexual abuse cases involve adolescent offenders and younger victims, many of whom are related.

As a practice, incest generally begins early in a child's life. The Harborview Report (Seattle) found that 22 percent of the victims of incest were between one and six years old; 40 percent were between seven and twelve; and 38 percent between thirteen and sixteen.[3] The tragedy with incest is that it begins at such a young age for most children that they are simply too young to understand its implications or to resist the advances of the molester.

Studies reveal that incest can begin as early as one or two years of age and continue long into one's adult years.[4] However, most cases involve girls molested by their fathers or stepfathers from about age nine until the girl is in her late teens.

Almost all the research done to date on incest shows that female victims outnumber male victims 10 to 1, with male victims generally being involved in homosexual activity.[5] Research has also shown that when male perpetrators have incestuous sex with male victims, it is not so much because of homosexual tendencies as it is the man's "taking whatever is available."[6] This is especially true of adolescent perpetrators.

Incest fills the home with jealousy, strife, and guilt. In father-daughter relationships, the daughter is often given favored treatment above the other children and even her mother. In some situations, the mother and daughter become highly competitive and in constant conflict. Often the daughter becomes rebellious as an older adolescent, and the mother becomes totally incapable of controlling her. Inside, the daughter knows she has closer access to her father than her mother does.

Most molesting fathers are themselves tragic figures. Some have been sexually frustrated and confused since their own adolescence. Others have wives who have sexually neglected or rejected them. They turn to a child because their potential for rejection is lower.

## CAN YOU FORGIVE ME?

Cathy was in her early forties when she caught her husband Bob and their fifteen-year-old daughter Julie in bed together. Hurt and confused, she blamed Julie for seducing her husband by "running around in her underwear."

Julie was devastated. It had been going on since she was eight. Initially it just involved touching. Later, it developed into a full relationship of intercourse. As she got into her teenage years, she realized this relationship was not normal but was too scared and embarrassed to tell anyone. She lived in constant fear that her father would make advances to her, so she tried to avoid him as much as she could.

Then they were alone in the house. Her mother had taken her brother to baseball practice and intended to go on an extended shopping spree. When she unexpectedly returned home to get her checkbook and credit cards, she walked in on them.

"At first she just stood there in total shock," Julie said. "Then she began screaming at me and hitting me. She called me every name you can imagine. My dad just sat there and let her do it."

"I felt so betrayed," Julie said. "It had been going on for years. She had to know something, but she had never tried to stop it. Whenever I tried to tell her, she just brushed it off. I really think she just tried to block it out of her mind."

"This time there was no blocking it out, was there?" I asked.

"No, she had to deal with it, so she took it out on me," Julie said. "My life became a living hell. She had failed to protect me; he had molested me; and now she was blaming the whole thing on me. That's why I finally went to a counselor at school. I couldn't take it anymore."

The family had been under professional counseling for some time when I first met them in Houston, Texas. Julie had committed her life to Christ in one of our crusades and wanted to know how she could ever forgive her parents. Her mother, Cathy, came with her to talk to one of our counselors who was trained in incest intervention. Afterward, they talked to me and told me what had happened.

As we talked it became clear that Julie really wanted to put this whole matter behind her and get on with the rest of her life. Cathy, however, was still struggling with it.

"You have to be willing to forgive Julie and your husband before you can deal with this," I suggested. "You can't live in the past forever."

"I want to," Cathy said, "but I feel I'm the one who failed her."

"You did," I interrupted, "by not listening to her and by not stopping it."

"I'm sorry, Julie," she said. "I just couldn't face it. I didn't want to believe it. I've really failed you as a mother."

"Maybe so," I suggested, "but it's never too late to start over."

Cathy looked at Julie and asked, "Will you forgive me, honey?"

"Yes, Mom, I sure will," Julie answered as they reached out to embrace each other, tears flowing down their cheeks as they cried, smiled, and talked, all at the same time.

"Now, we'll have to work on forgiving your father too," Cathy said, and Julie nodded approvingly.

It was not an easy process for any of them. Julie still had great fears and a general uneasiness around her father for some time after that. Cathy struggled for months with bitterness and humiliation. At times, she even questioned her own sexuality as a woman. All of them were uptight around each other. But little by little they began to make progress.

Mother and daughter took united action and confronted Bob, demanding a change in his behavior. Stunned by the confrontation, he immediately ceased any further advances and seemed to become a different person. With the help of some long-range counseling, they were able to make total *and* complete restitution with each other. With wise caution, professional help and the grace of God, they have been able to resume a normal family life.

## WHAT GOES WRONG?

Fathers who become incestuously involved with their daughters usually have symbiotic personalities by which they seek to satisfy their need for closeness and intimacy through sex. "Some are bullying, others are persuasive, some are shy and play on sympathy and misguided loyalty, still others use alcohol to express their dependency and then, claiming loss of control, seek satisfaction of their needs through sex," wrote Blair and Rita Justice.[7]

In each case the father experiences isolation and distance from other people, including his wife. Sexual rejection complicates the problem but is not the only cause. The Justices categorized incestuous fathers as one of four types:

1. Tyrant
2. Rationalizer
3. Introvert
4. Alcoholic

While their outward personality characteristics may appear to vary, inwardly, "Each type shares the inability to reach out to others, to establish closeness, to get attention and affection through daily human contacts."[8] Many incestuous fathers appear strong and protective, but inwardly "they are starved for affection and hungry for someone who will nurture and comfort them."[9]

Several psychological reverses take place during incest between fathers and daughters. In some cases the father thinks of his daughter as "belonging" to him and thereby rationalizes the relationship as being better than going outside the home for it. Some fathers try to assume the role of "teacher" in order to prepare the daughter for marriage. I suspect this attitude is often also taken by older women who make sexual advances toward younger boys. Some incestuous fathers cling to the past, wanting their daughters to remain their "baby girls." They resist their growing up, dating, or moving away from home. In most of these cases the father becomes unnaturally possessive of his daughter.

The Justices list several characteristics of incestuous father-daughter relationships:[10]

Blurring of Parent-Child Roles:
    Father takes "child" position
    Mother takes "child" position
    Daughter takes role of "mother" and "wife" in family
    Father acts as suitor to daughter
    Mother acts as rival to daughter
Overpossessiveness by Father:
    Father jealous of daughter's peers
    Father often alone with daughter
    Father favors daughter over other children
    Siblings jealous of daughter favored by father
    Father resents daughter's dating
Effects on Daughter:
    Daughter has poor self-image
    Daughter depressed and withdrawn
    Daughter uninvolved in school activities
    Daughter very secretive
    Daughter excessively seductive
    Daughter and mother not close
    Daughter often rebels against mother's authority
Effects on Mother:
    Mother outwardly aloof and uninvolved
    Mother inwardly fearful and suspicious
    Mother blocks out reality by denial
Effects on Husband-Wife:
    Surface relationship
    Little shared intimacy
    Little sexual involvement
    Arguments over the daughter

## EFFECTS ON THE FAMILY

Incestuous families become very poor role models for children. When a daughter has sex with her father, she gains a special power over him. She is both a child and an equal at the same time. Role confusion results when she is not certain whether she is functioning as a daughter or as a lover. The mother in an incestuous family becomes both parent and rival to her daughter, often provoking angry outbursts from the daughter toward herself, whom she views as failing both her and her father. In such cases, there is a great deal of transferred guilt from the daughter to the mother.

Other children in the family are confused as well about lines of authority in the family. The "unchosen" siblings resent the "chosen" one. Rivalry, favoritism, and internal conflict often result. The children in an incestuous family see a poor example of how to parent. They feel that their parents do not set limits fairly because one child receives most of the father's attention. They also sense unconsciously that the parent is looking to the child for nurture instead of the parents nurturing the children.

In most cases an incestuous relationship ends when someone demands that it end. This demand is usually made by the daughter who refuses to continue the relationship when she is older. In some cases it is made when the relationship is discovered by the mother or another family member. And in a few cases, it ends when the matter is reported to the proper authorities.

"One night I just got up the nerve to say no," said Tiffany, a sixteen year old.

"It ended for me when I went away to college," added Tonya. "I just would not agree to it after I came home on break."

"I had to leave home," said Betty. "I just couldn't deal with it, and I couldn't get him to stop."

Diane and I spoke to a group of teenage girls in Orlando,

Florida. Each one had an incestuous relationship with her father, and they were trying to help each other deal with it.

"What advice would you give someone else in this situation?" asked Diane.

"I'd tell them to tell someone outside the home," answered Tonya. "If that doesn't work, then move out!"

"I think everyone involved needs help," added Tiffany. "I know we all did. My mom was devastated and resentful. My dad was ashamed and he was devastated too. I was just glad it was over, but I still had to learn to forgive and forget. It took awhile, but it's working now."

The immediate and long-term effects of incest on the family are traumatic indeed. There is the horror and embarrassment of exposure, stressful legal involvements, blame, disbelief, false accusation, possible divorce, and the potential separation of family members.

The long-range consequences of incest to the daughter include:

1. guilt
2. depression
3. low self-esteem
4. feeling uniquely different
5. sexual dysfunction
6. distrust
7. self-destructive behavior

"I went through it all," Laura said. "I just wanted to run away and die. I had so much pain and guilt, I couldn't face anyone. I'd get loaded and hope I'd never wake up again. Later, when I got married, I would just freeze up sexually. I couldn't stand the thought of sex because it reminded me of my father."

"It was just the opposite for me," said Joanne. "I ran wild with guys, letting them do anything to me they wanted to because I thought it would get me over my dad. I feel like he actually drove me to have sex with guys just to escape from him."

These are all heart-breaking stories of real people who have suffered one of life's great tragedies. It is bad enough to bring wrong on yourself, but when it is perpetrated by others, it is even more difficult to take.

You can't spend the rest of your life condemning yourself or holding on to internal bitterness. Only as you learn to forgive and forget can you shake off the past and move on with your life. You do not have to remain the victim of someone else's sin.

## KIDS DO IT TOO

Donnie was small for his age of thirteen and older kids were always picking on him. Every trip to and from school became a major trauma in his life. When he was in the eighth grade some older boys beat him up and forced him to have oral sex with them.

He was so humiliated that he would not tell anyone what happened. Every time he saw the same guys again, he felt sick to his stomach and rushed off to avoid them. He became tense and nervous. His grades fell and he withdrew from other kids.

Donnie heard me tell my life story in his school, and afterward, he asked to talk to me. Donnie poured his heart out about what had happened to him.

"Does this mean I'm a homosexual, Jay?" he asked, bewildered.

"Not at all!" I replied confidently. "Do you want to be a homosexual?"

"No!" he said.

"Did you like what happened?" I asked.

"No!"

"Then that's your answer. Just because somebody did something wrong to you, doesn't mean you were wrong."

We talked together for some time and then we prayed together. Donnie gave his life to Christ. "Thanks, Jay, this really helped," he said. "I can tell you understand."

Donnie wrote to me several times after that. He eventually

graduated from high school and went on to a Baptist college in the Midwest to study for the ministry. God had set him free from his past and made him free to serve Him.

Tragically, we humans tend to pervert and pollute everything God gives us. We have irresponsibly polluted this earth, but even worse, we have polluted each other. Perhaps you have been a victim or a perpetrator of sexual sin. The time to stop is now! It's never too late, and you are never too old to quit. This side of eternity, no one is beyond the touch of God's grace at any time in his life.

Whether you were the victim of sexual child abuse or the perpetrator of it, you can rise above your past. Satan wants you to believe that you are dirty and vile. He wants you to believe you cannot be forgiven and that no one will ever want to be married to you. All of that is a lie.

Your potential for a successful marriage may have been damaged by your experience, but it has certainly not been eliminated. You are not the first person to face this kind of pain. Millions of men and women have been hurt in similar ways as you have been hurt. They too have had to overcome their past and build a new life for themselves.

Jim was a child molester from Los Angeles. He had been hooked on hard-core pornography for years. His homosexual attraction to young teenage boys had become progressively worse. He had been charged with exposure and sodomy twice before he finally broke down and confessed his sin to his parents and pastor.

When the pastor first asked me to talk to him, I was a little apprehensive. I had endured a bad experience myself as a young teenager from an older stepbrother. I wondered if I could really love Jim and forgive him for what he had done.

"He's here," the pastor announced abruptly. "I'll bring him in to meet you."

When he appeared in the doorway, he was thin and slightly built. He hung his head down with shame and stammered as he talked. Clearly he was no criminal sadist or child hater. He was insecure and desperately wanted to be loved and accepted.

"How did this get started, Jim?" I asked.

"When I was a kid, somebody did it to me," he replied sheepishly. "From there it just kept getting worse until I started doing it to others."

As we talked I could sense the brokenness and repentance in his voice. He had been publicly humiliated and had served time in jail for his sins. He was currently under psychiatric care as well.

"I really don't want to live like this any more," he said. "I've given my life to Christ and asked Him to cleanse me and change me. I know it won't be easy to break this addiction in my life, but I sure am willing to try."

I shared with Jim the importance of renewing his mind as well as disciplining his body. "You need to memorize scripture and meditate on it constantly," I suggested.

He promised to do the memorizing I suggested and when I saw him again the next year, he had memorized almost five hundred verses of scripture.

"I've made a complete break with it, Jay," he said. "I got rid of everything associated with my old life, even a couple of friends with whom I could no longer associate."

As we stood talking a year later, he seemed a totally different person. His attitude and mannerisms had changed drastically. Christ was now obviously in control of his life.

When we parted company, Jim looked at me and said, "Thanks for everything, Jay."

Without hesitation, I said, "Hey, that's O.K. I love you, man."

Suddenly, I realized that God had been working in my life as well.

## Chapter 10

# Rape:
# Sexual
# Violence

"I'LL BE RIGHT back, Penny," called Susan as she went out the door to run to the store.

"That's O.K.," Penny shouted back, "I'm going to do the wash."

The two girls had been roommates for about six months and had enjoyed every moment together. They had several things in common which added to the warmth of their friendship. Both were recent college graduates in their early twenties, who had just started new jobs in Houston.

Weekends were always busy times for the girls, because they had to catch up on all their housework. Penny often worried about Susan because she wasn't used to living in a big city.

"You trust everybody too much," Penny told her often. "You need to lock your car and quit running all over town at night."

"Oh, you worry too much," Susan said. "I'll be all right."

I suppose that's why Penny was so unprepared when she carried the load of clothes into the laundry room. A man in his early thirties grabbed her from behind and put a gun to her head.

"Get down on the floor," he demanded, "and take off your clothes."

Penny just stood there in stunned silence trying to say no, but the words wouldn't come out of her mouth.

"I remember trying to shake my head 'no'," she told me later, "but he thought I was trying to get loose. He pushed me to the floor and the bundle of clothes went sprawling everywhere. I was so frightened I couldn't move. It was as if time stood still . . . like I wasn't really there . . . like I was just watching the whole thing happen on television."

"He started taking off my clothes," Penny continued, "and I just let him. He kept the gun right in my face the whole time. I felt like screaming, but I couldn't. I can't even remember what he looked like. I just kept thinking about all those clothes strewn all over the floor."

"Before I could even think about resisting," she went on, "it was all over. Then I kept thinking, 'Now he's going to kill me.' I remember closing my eyes and praying, 'God, please don't let him kill me.' When I opened my eyes he was going out the door."

Rape is a terrible, emotionally traumatic experience for any woman. Although everyone responds to it differently, rape is still a devastating experience. It is a violation of one's inner dignity, security, sanctity and often, virginity.[1]

Few women remain calm during a rape. Some panic and go into hysteria; others fight back and struggle to get free; some, like Penny, lapse into denial and try to pretend the whole thing is not happening. Afterward, some women erroneously blame themselves for not fighting back, and others second-guess themselves, questioning whether trying to fight back may not have made the whole thing worse.

Whenever we try to help someone who has been raped, we need to express a great deal of understanding, warmth, and concern. They need our support and encouragement, not an endless barrage of suspicious or curious questions.

Helen Benedict warned that many people still do not understand "that rape is a violent crime [in which] the victim of rape carries a special burden."[2] Benedict observed that, though the victim has probably endured the worst experience of her life, many of the people in her life don't really understand just how serious it has been.

> When someone . . . is met with leers from the police or doctors and hears jokes and impatient comments from friends, she feels utterly alone, as if the whole world has turned against her. One minute she was herself, minding her own business like anyone else, a private being with her own, small life. The next she is an object to be first brutalized and then sneered at.[3]

What every concerned person needs to realize is that rape *hurts*. It hurts while it is happening, and it hurts long after it is over. It damages one's self-respect and self-confidence. It leaves a woman with fear and dread for her immediate and long-range health and safety. Virtually every female rape victim experiences some kind of emotional disturbance.[4]

## MYTHS AND REALITIES

By definition rape is any sexual act that is forced upon another person. It may include sexual intercourse as well as other forms of sexual assault that don't go "all the way." Legal definitions are more technical and are generally limited to vaginal rape.

Helen Benedict stated that the "deepest horror of being raped lies in the fear of being killed."[5] Then she adds that this fear is followed by the devastating humiliation and terror of knowing that one's personal privacy has been forcibly violated. Other fears of such things as venereal disease, pregnancy, sexual dysfunction, AIDS, or fear of future assault come afterward.

Once a woman has been raped, it is difficult for her to believe she will ever be the same again. Many victims of rape blame themselves for taking risks that may seem to have invited intrusion. However, in most cases, the woman was a totally innocent and unsuspecting victim.[6]

Benedict listed five myths about rape that must be dispelled in order to properly understand what has happened.

*Myth 1: Rape is sex.* In reality, rape is an act of violence against a woman, in which sex is the weapon. Rape is not just another sexual experience that doesn't hurt the victim any more than sex does. It is an act of violence and abuse in which the victim's life and health are endangered.

*Myth 2: Rape is lust.* Psychological studies now reveal that the majority of rapists are provoked by anger or revenge. These rapes are premeditated attacks to express power over the victim or anger toward women in general. Only in the case of the sadistic rapist is violence associated with sexual pleasure.[7]

*Myth 3: Rapists are weirdos.* The fact is that a rapist can be just about anybody. There is generally no such thing as a seedy social reject lurking in dark alleys looking for women. One study has revealed that 60 percent of the assailants were known to the victims. Thus, rapists can be almost anyone: doctors, lovers, therapists, relatives, teachers, bosses, or boyfriends.

*Myth 4: Women provoke rape.* While this may happen at times because of a woman's dress or behavior, it is the exception, not the rule. Benedict stated, "Because rapists are believed to be motivated by lust, their victims are believed to have enticed them."[8] This myth then becomes terribly destructive for the victim, who often unnecessarily blames herself for provoking the crime. It is interesting, however, to note that lustful provocation is almost *never* cited in cases involving a male's being raped by another male.

*Myth 5: Only bad women are raped.* Most people realize this myth is not true, but it is often the basis of the courtroom defense of rapists. The attorney often attempts to paint the woman as a bad person who, by implication, deserved to get raped. The truth is that no one, male or female, ever deserved to be raped.

Rape is both a crime and a sin. It is an act of total selfish indulgence at the expense of another human being. As such, it deserves the strongest legal penalties as a deterrent to a self-indulgent society.

## JODY'S STORY

Jody was a stewardess for a major airline headquartered in Dallas. She had committed her life to Christ in one of our crusades there and asked to talk to Diane.

"Can I help with something?" Diane asked her.

"Yes, I think you can," Jody replied. "Now that I'm a Christian I have a serious question about something that happened in my past."

"What's that?" Diane asked.

"Well, about two years ago," Jody said, "I was raped in the airport parking lot on the way to my car." She proceeded to explain some of the details and then asked, "Will God forgive me for this?"

"He doesn't have to forgive you," Diane said, "because you didn't do anything wrong!"

"I guess what I'm really trying to ask," Jody said, "is whether He can cleanse me so I can be the woman He wants me to be."

"Sure He can," Diane responded confidently. "That's what scripture promises."

As they talked together, Diane told Jody about the wonderful grace of God, by which He accepts us just as we are in life.

"You don't have to prove anything to God, Jody," Diane stated. "He's on your side."

"Can I still have a happy marriage and a Christian home?" Jody asked.

"Of course," Diane said. "Your ability to build a Christian home and family is in no way limited by what happened in your past."

"I guess I've always felt like it was my fault," Jody said.

"The other girls were always warning me about being alone out there, and I just didn't take it seriously."

"Hey," Diane interrupted, "even women who take it seriously get raped. You can't keep on blaming yourself for what happened."

"I guess I still have a lot of fears about it," Jody confessed.

"So do a lot of women. But you can't spend the rest of your life in doubt and fear."

Then Jody hesitated for a moment, as if she were reluctant to ask the next question.

"I really hate that guy," Jody said. "Now that I'm a Christian, do I have to forgive him?"

"What did Jesus say about forgiveness?" Diane asked.

"He said to forgive even your enemies," she responded reluctantly.

"Is he your enemy?" Diane asked further.

"Yes," she said abruptly, "he sure is!"

Learning to forgive anyone who hurts us is not easy, but forgiving a rapist is virtually impossible apart from the grace of God in our lives. Yet forgiving our worst enemies is part of the healing process that is necessary in our lives if we are to overcome the hurts inflicted on us by others.

## REACTIONS TO RAPE

Everybody reacts differently to threats of violence, including rape. There is no set, right response. However, most rape victims acknowledge that these reactions are typical of those who have been raped.

1. *Fear of Dying*. The initial fear of every woman while she is being raped is that she will also be killed. The vast majority of rape victims are threatened with violent weapons such as guns or knives. As one victim put it, "If he is crazy enough to do this, he's crazy enough to kill me."

2. *Physical Pain*. Once a person has survived rape with his or her life, the next issue is to deal with the painful physical results of the rape. Physical reactions may include trauma, loss

of appetite, nausea, cuts, bleeding, bruises, or even broken bones. In addition to these, women have a fear of pregnancy.

3. *Psychological Pain*. For many, this is the greatest pain of all and takes the longest to heal. During this time the victim often experiences fluctuating emotional mood swings, depression, loss of self-esteem, insecurity, phobias, fears, nervous or compulsive habits, and loss of sexual desire.

4. *Sexual Dysfunction*. Many women have a difficult time initiating a normal sex life after rape. Some fear being physically hurt again and others merely associate sex with what happened during the rape. Virgins who are raped may especially fear that they cannot develop a normal sex life afterward.

5. *Revenge*. Many rape victims experience revengeful dreams or nightmares about their experience. They often become exasperated with the nagging persistence of these dreams, but they may well be part of the recovery process. Ultimately the rage within us must turn to more positive and constructive responses.

6. *Flashbacks*. Just when the victims seem to have put the emotional consequences of the ordeal behind them, they may experience flashbacks of fear or anxiety. Remember that these are not recurrences of the actual experience itself. Remind yourself that the ordeal is over and that you are now safe.

7. *Embarrassment*. Many people are too embarrassed to admit they have been raped. This is why it is so difficult to get people to prosecute rapists. It also prevents the authorities from compiling accurate records on the frequency of rape. Even years later personal embarrassment can keep a victim from speaking up and helping someone else who has been through the same thing.

## WHEN IT HAPPENS

Most victims do not have time to think through their reaction to a rape. Often it is over before they even think to respond to it. When there is time to think, consider these possible reactions.

1. *Pray.* That's right, pray—out loud. That lets the rapist know that he is violating God's righteousness as well as your body. Many rapists have been known to leave a potential victim alone when the victim began calling upon God for deliverance.

2. *Call out.* The police tell potential victims in populated areas to call out for help. Even if people are afraid to respond, your calling out threatens the rapist with intervention from others.

3. *Run.* If at all possible, run away to someone who can help you, like a neighbor or policeman, or run into a public place where the rapist can be seen and identified.

4. *Resist.* Rapists tend to prey on victims they consider to be weak. They rarely attack a woman with a briefcase and a hat, who appears to be a successful or dominant business-woman. Resistance lets him know this is not going to come easy and may cause him to give up.

5. *Remain calm.* Obviously this may be hard to do. But many women have testified that by remaining calm and even trying to express sympathy to the rapist they were able to talk him out of it. If you can't run, resist or talk him out of it, sub-mission may be necessary to save your life.

While some women have been fortunate to escape rape, others have not. What works for one person may not work for another. Never judge anyone's response to a rape. It is a lot easier to say what you would do when you are not confronted with the actual threat yourself.

When a rape does occur, several steps are vital:

1. *Get to a safe place.* Don't stay alone in the place you were raped. Get to a friend's house, go to the hospital, or go to the police. Call the Rape Crisis Hotline in your community.

2. *Keep the evidence.* If at all possible keep the clothes you were wearing when you were raped and any other pertinent evidence to prosecute the rapist.

3. *Don't wash.* Though this may be difficult to follow, go to the hospital first. Let them clean you up properly. They can also verify the fact that you were raped better before you wash up.

4. *Find help*. You may be afraid to ask for help or you may be embarrassed to admit you have been raped. Some women try to tell themselves nothing really serious happened as a form of psychological denial. Others don't want to go through the legal hassles.

Helen Benedict said, "Choosing to tell about the rape is not always simple."[9] But you need to be listened to, sympathized with, and believed. At first you may be afraid to tell your husband, boyfriend or parents, but you need to tell someone who can help.

5. *Seek counsel*. Don't try to carry this burden alone. You need to get proper professional counseling to help you get through this ordeal properly. Sometimes even spouses or friends don't understand what you have been through. Rape crisis centers are usually affiliated with hospitals or women's centers. Their workers are trained to sympathize with rape victims and to provide care and understanding that will help you cope with the ordeal.

6. *Report the crime*. Many women are reluctant to report their rape. Some are unwilling to talk about it. Others do not want the hassle of legal prosecution. Some fear they will not get a sympathetic response. My advice is take somebody with you, preferably a man. Remain calm as you make the report and do everything you can to identify the rapist. You owe it to his next victim.

7. *Get a physical examination*. Don't be afraid to get a thorough examination. You need to know if any physical damage was done. You also need to take precautions against the possibility of venereal disease or AIDS. Sometimes tests for such possibilities have to be done even weeks later. Don't avoid these. Pretending nothing is wrong won't make any problem go away.

## RECOVERY

Emotional recovery from the trauma of rape can take anywhere from six months to six years to accomplish.[10] However long the process, victims need love, support, and understanding in order to resume a normal life. As a husband, relative, or friend, you can provide that support better than anyone.

Giving support can be more difficult than we imagine. Some people wrongly try to play down the whole thing as not all that bad. Others foolishly blame it on the sovereignty of God with "well, He must have meant it for good." Some men, even husbands, get unnaturally turned on by the whole thing as though it were sexy.

To the victim, there is nothing good or sexy about what has happened. To them it is a violation of their dignity, privacy, and security—a threat to their very lives. When we don't understand that, we only add insult to injury.

Several factors are crucial if the victim is to renew a normal life after the crisis has passed.

1. *Recovery takes time.* Nobody rebounds from something as traumatic as rape overnight. Recovery takes time because the victim often feels unsafe and fearful. There may be many dark moments afterward, but your life has not been totally ruined. There is still time and hope for a better future. Remember, recovery takes patience and courage.

2. *Safety must be rebuilt.* Rape shatters a victim's feeling of safety and normality. Afterward, you may be filled with unwarranted fears about men, sex, night, the city, or a hundred other things. You have been unfortunate, but that doesn't mean everything has gone wrong. You may realize the world isn't as safe as you thought, but that doesn't mean you are in danger every moment. Safety and security must be re-established. You may need to move, or you may want to take a self-defense course. Whatever you do, go about *actively* protecting yourself and rebuilding your confidence.

3. *Don't keep blaming yourself.* Some victims relive the experience over and over, condemning themselves for taking chances. "It wouldn't have happened if . . . " is a common reaction. If you took an unnecessary risk, like hitch-hiking or walking alone at night, learn your lesson and don't do it again. Self-doubt and self-blame cannot eliminate what has hap-

pened. But taking proper precautions in the future can help keep you safe.

4. *Keep your time structured*. Don't sit around endlessly brooding over what happened. Fill your time with positive, confidence-building activities: treat yourself to something special; visit your friends; go on a trip. You may be exhausted from the whole ordeal and need a vacation. Don't try to go on as though nothing has happened. Something did happen— something terrible. Face it, talk about it, deal with it, and get on with the rest of your life.

5. *Seek counseling*. Talk to your pastor or a professional Christian counselor. Crisis intervention counseling is especially helpful in dealing with your initial fears and traumas. If long-range fears persist, see a counselor and get them resolved. Make sure the counselor has an adequate background for dealing with sexual assault victims. Proper therapy will give you guidance to recovery.

6. *Communicate with your husband*. In a sense, he will feel victimized also. Let him in on your hurts, fears, and feelings. Don't reject him when he tries to express his love and concern. Couple therapy can also be very beneficial. It can help open better communication and dissolve the myths that stand in the way of total recovery.

7. *Talk to God*. This is a very important step because many rape victims feel God has let them down. Others may actually feel that they have let Him down. Either way, one's relationship to God must be resolved through all this. Remember, God is not the author of sin: He did not order this sinful act against you. He still loves you as much as He ever did, and your life is still in His hands. So don't blame God for what went wrong. Instead, trust Him to help you recover.

8. *Forgive your assailant*. I know this is a tough step, but it is a necessary one. Forgiving leads to forgetting the hurt, and that's what you need. Forgiving, however, does not mean letting the rapist go free. Legal prosecution may be necessary to stop him from victimizing someone else. But forgiveness is what will set your spirit free. You don't have to remain the victim of someone else's sin.

9. *Prosecute if possible.* When positive identity can be made, the perpetrator should be prosecuted for his own good and the good of society. Remember, rapists are out of control, and incarceration may be necessary to prevent them from harming others.

10. *Go on with your life.* You can't keep living in the past. Settle all the unfinished business related to this unpleasant episode, and then move on with the rest of your life. Time is a great healer and it will help push this incident further to the back of your mind. Although you will never totally forget your experience, you will no longer have to live in daily fear of it either.

The future is your destiny, not the past. Rebuilding trust and communication is vital to your recovery. As you work through the trauma of this experience, learn to lean on God, friends, and relatives. They love you and care about you.

## A WORD ABOUT SEXUALITY

Remember that rape is an act of violence, not an act of sex. But because sex is associated with it, many victims feel their sexuality has been violated. They fear renewing sex with their spouse. Sometimes victims put off the whole issue of sexual intercourse for several months. Others try to start again, but the whole process, or some aspect of it, reminds them of the ordeal of the rape.

When you do start to make love again, though, go slowly, emphasizing the gentle aspects of love-making. Approaching sex gradually and cautiously at first will help you rebuild your normal desire. The greatest battle with sexual recovery is in your own mind. Keep reminding yourself that sex and rape are not the same thing. Everyone is different and one woman's experience can't be made the rule for all. But given enough time, you can overcome all these obstacles and resume a normal, loving sexual relationship with your husband.

There is no evidence at all that rape changes a person's sexual orientation, even rape by a member of the same sex. And unless there has been physical damage or venereal disease from the rape, you should be able to resume a normal sexual life.

Let me also say a word to teenagers who have been raped. Rape is not the end of your virginity. It may technically mean you are no longer a virgin physically, but you can still remain a virgin spiritually. God does not hold you responsible for an action done by someone else against your will. You can still lead a positive and productive Christian life. What has happened does not have to limit your future, your marriage, or your family.

Teens tend to worry about five major factors related to rape:

1. *Parents*. Most kids are afraid to tell their parents for fear they will get angry, accuse them, or restrict them. You may be reluctant to tell them, but you must be honest with them. There is no way they can begin to help you if they don't know what has happened. This goes for guys who have been sexually assaulted or girls who have been raped. If you are afraid of your parents' reaction, take a teacher, counselor, or youth pastor with you.

2. *Friends*. You may be fortunate enough to have friends who are understanding or caring. If so, they can be a wonderful source of help and support. However, most teens are reluctant to tell their friends because of shame or embarrassment. That's why you need to tell your parents. Your friends don't need to know if you don't want them to know.

3. *School*. Kids who have been sexually raped or assaulted often fear returning to school. Fearing they will be misunderstood, they think they will be called names like "whore" or "gay" or "queer." Schools can be places where news like this spreads fast; nevertheless, it is best to return to school as soon as possible. If no one knows, school might become a place of safety and relief. But even if people do know, the sooner you return to normal activities, the sooner you will feel normal yourself.

4. *Shame*. Feeling ashamed of what happened is normal. But staying that way is not. Dropping out of school or going to the other extreme and becoming an overachiever isn't necessary

to compensate for what has happened. You don't have to do either. Just be yourself.

5. *Sex*. You may be questioning how the rape will affect your own sexuality in the future. Remember, rape is not sex and it does not change your sexual identity or orientation. One teenage victim put it this way: "Comparing rape to sex is like comparing a punch in the mouth to a kiss."[11]

Whatever has gone wrong can be made right. But you must take the right steps to correct it. Learn to keep your guard up in the future, and don't put yourself in vulnerable situations. Many girls foolishly get drunk on alcohol or high on drugs and hope the guys will leave them alone. But this actually makes them vulnerable, and they lose self-control, after which almost anything can happen. Many a girl has been gang raped while in such a condition.

If you want to avoid rape, don't take unnecessary risks. Don't walk or drive alone at night. Stay out of isolated places, even in the daytime. Don't date guys who are known to try to force girls into having sex. All these habits just add to your vulnerability.

But remember, you can take all the precautions in the world and still get assaulted. It is not your fault that someone sinned against you—they are the violator, not you. God promises to take vengeance on all who do so and make them repay (see 1 Thessalonians 4:3–6). God promises that He will take care of the rapist. You don't have to strike back. You simply need to take care of yourself.

As you work through all the effects of the sexual assault on your life, realize that you can have a completely normal and happy life again. God still loves you as much as He ever did, and He still plans to use you to serve Him—perhaps even more powerfully than ever!

## Chapter 11

# Abortion: The Wrong Choice

EVER SINCE THE Supreme Court legalized abortion on demand in 1973, we have killed millions of unborn babies in this country with the excuse that they are "unwanted pregnancies." Many a would-be mother later regretted her decision, but it was too late.

Since the 1960s abortion has become an increasingly popular method of birth control. By 1980, 37 percent of all pregnancies ended in abortion.[1] The total number of abortions rose from 485,000 in 1971 to over 1,500,000 by 1983. Today abortion remains a significant option for thousands of women who just don't want to be bothered with caring for another human life.

One recent study revealed that those who had abortions or favored legalized abortions were also more likely to favor euthanasia, infanticide, suicide, homosexuality, and the use of drugs and alcohol.[2] This group also expressed a lower satisfaction with life in general. One generation's frustration has become another generation's elimination.

## THE CULT OF SELF-WORSHIP

Ours is a generation caught up in the cult of self-worship. Because we want whatever pleases us, we have a totally undisci-

plined and unrestrained attitude about sex. This often leads to
unplanned pregnancies which are, in turn, conveniently eliminated by abortion.

In this self-centered culture, a woman is encouraged to as-
sert her "right" to an abortion by denying her baby's right to
life. The mother's right to convenience cancels the baby's right
to life. By choosing abortion, the mother also denies the humanity of her unborn child.

The increasing secularization of our society since the
1940s has brought us to a point of moral neutrality today. People simply don't want to take a position on controversial moral
issues. We would just as soon go to the beach and forget the
whole thing.

In his powerful book *What is Secular Humanism?* Professor James Hitchcock of St. Louis University, raised this important observation:

> Modern Supreme Court decisions strongly reflect the
> assumptions of eighteenth-century rationalists,
> especially in their suspicion of religion as a divisive
> force in public life . . . Such opinions represent not
> careful judicial thought but the prejudices of the judges.
> These prejudices have now been enshrined in court
> decisions.[3]

Since 1973 Americans have placed their own personal
convenience over the lives of the unborn. As a result, the unborn have been treated as non-humans. This trend is reflected
in abortion-related terminology, such as calling the baby a
P.O.C. (product of conception). Even the use of the term *fetus*
is generally taken to mean something less than human.

The most tragic victims of abortion are usually pregnant
teenagers who are quickly told to "get rid of it." Their natural
fear of embarrassment and the possible reactions of their parents have caused many teenagers to opt for abortion without
even considering the consequences.

## NEW LIVES FOR OLD

One night while I was preaching in a church in Alabama, two blonde girls came forward during the invitation. Instead of standing at the altar while I waited for others to come as well, one of them reached up and tugged at the leg of my pants to get my attention.

"Can I ask you something?" she said, as the music continued to play.

"Sure, what is it?" I asked as I stooped down on the platform to hear her better.

"Is what you said really true?" she asked. "Can God really forgive us?"

"Yes, He can!" I responded confidently. "If you will repent of your sin and turn to Him, He will not reject you. God is in the people business. He loves, forgives, corrects, and restores. He gives new lives for old ones."

"Well, I've done something pretty serious," she added as the tears began to cascade down her face. "I've killed my baby. I just can't believe I did it, but I was scared and the people at the clinic just told me to go ahead—so I did."

I walked down the steps to get to the floor where they were both standing as our crusade song leader continued the invitation.

The first girl introduced herself and her friend, who said, "I did the same thing. We've never told anyone but each other."

As we talked together, I discovered that they were both fifteen-year-old, high-school sophomores. Each had gotten pregnant early in her freshman year in separate incidents. Later they had confided in each other about what they had done.

"I really didn't want to do it," the first one said, "but I got drunk at a party and got carried away. I'm not even sure who got me pregnant."

"My situation was different," said the other. "My boyfriend got me pregnant and told me to get an abortion or he was through with me. After I did it, we broke up anyway. Now, I feel terrible about what I've done."

"You know," I said, "sin always has consequences, and sometimes they are not very pleasant. When I was a kid, I did a lot of things of which I'm not proud. They cost me a lot of hurt and they hurt others too." They both listened intently as I talked. I went on to explain that God does not excuse our sin, but He is more than willing to forgive it and help us to start all over again.

"There is nothing you can do to bring your babies back," I said. "But you can turn away from the lifestyle that led to this and turn your lives over to Christ."

They both indicated that was what they wanted to do. At the end of the invitation I prayed with those who had come to commit themselves to Christ and then referred them to our counselors for personal follow-up of their decisions. Both of the teenagers were counseled by kind, godly women who understood their guilt and fears. Their counselors prayed with them to seek Christ's forgiveness and then gave them guidelines on how to live a successful Christian life.

The girls left that night with the joy of the Lord on their faces. Their pasts were forgiven and their futures were clean slates. As they left the church I met them briefly in the lobby and encouraged them to claim the verse in Isaiah 1:18: "Come now, and let us reason together, saith the Lord: though your sins be as scarlet, they shall be as white as snow; though they be red like crimson, they shall be as wool."

As they left, I wondered what would become of them. *Did they really mean business?* I questioned. *Will there be a difference in their lives?*

Years later I learned that one of them had graduated from high school and attended a Christian college where she met and married a young man who was studying for the ministry. The other had also attended a church-related college and then became a counselor in a pro-life teenage crisis pregnancy center. God's grace had touched them both and set them on a new and wonderful course of life.

## IT DOESN'T END AT THE CLINIC

Last year alone, more than 1.5 million unborn children were aborted in our nation. Many, if not most, of the mothers were teenagers, only slightly more than children themselves. Too young to face such a crisis alone, they turn to friends, teachers, and counselors for advice. Unfortunately, the vast majority are referred to abortion clinics where the whole problem is disposed of in a few minutes. But the consequences can last a lifetime.

One girl told my wife and me that it doesn't end at the clinic. "As I walked out of there," she said, "I had a great sense of relief at first. I had hidden this whole thing from my parents and friends. Now, nobody would ever know, I thought. But I knew, and that was enough to torment me."

Guilt plagues those women who have selfishly decided to terminate a pregnancy because it would interfere with their lives. Yet, most who abort refuse to deal with this issue. They want to brush over it as though it were nothing more than self-imposed trauma. Scripture makes it clear, however, that guilt is real. It comes when we have violated a known standard of right and wrong. For most of us, murdering an unborn child is wrong, and we know it.

Part of my responsibility as an evangelist is to uphold the standard of God's righteousness. But an equal responsibility of my ministry is to extend His mercy and grace to fallen sinners. Whenever a preacher loses sight of that, he loses sight of what his ministry is all about. I cannot undo the wrong that others have done, but I don't have to hold it against them for the rest of their lives. They know they have failed, and they are desperately looking for forgiveness and hope. I am convinced that God wants us to be His instruments to give others that hope.

## FINDING A BETTER WAY

In his national best-seller *If I Should Die Before I Wake,* Jerry Falwell wrestled with this issue of abortion.[4] He knew that many would question a ministry to pregnant girls. There was a time when society looked upon unwed pregnant teens as wayward or delinquent. But today there are too many ordinary kids involved to hide them behind a demeaning label that really says, "We don't have to care."

Dr. Falwell wrote, "These girls need to experience the love of Christ through the love of a caring Christian community."[5] We cannot preach against abortion without providing a positive alternative, as Falwell has through his Godparent homes.

Jill was a pastor's daughter who had just graduated from high school. She got pregnant during the summer and was faced with telling her parents before she went off to college in the fall.

"I just can't tell them, Jay," she said to me after a service in their church.

"What are you going to do?" I asked.

"I can't get an abortion," she replied. "That just isn't right."

"Then don't you think you are going to have to tell your folks? You can't just go away to college and hope nobody notices!"

"I guess you're right," she said reluctantly. "Will you go with me, Jay?"

"Sure," I said, "let's talk to them tonight."

Jill's parents were devastated. At first her father seemed more concerned about himself than his daughter. He said he would have to quit the church and leave the ministry. But he eventually came to his senses.

"We love you, Jill," he said, "and while this hurts, it's not the end. Of course, we will stand by you, no matter what."

In time, the three of them were weeping and hugging each other. Compassion overruled criticism, and they began to rebuild at that difficult moment. Eventually Jill went to a maternity home, had the baby, and gave it up for adoption. Although she lost a year out of school, she saved a precious baby who deserved a chance at life.

## WHAT IS AT STAKE IN THE ABORTION DEBATE?

The ultimate issue is that of life itself. Life begins at conception, and terminating that conception terminates another life as willfully and deliberately as murder. In their epic work *Whatever Happened to the Human Race?* Christian philosopher Francis Schaeffer and pediatric surgeon C. Everett Koop stated: "Cultures can be judged in many ways, but eventually every nation in every age must be judged by this test: *How did it treat people?*"[6]

They argued that the abortion of the innocent unborn is an issue which has been thrust upon our culture by the courts and has pushed us to the edge of a great moral abyss. Once we capitulate on the life of the unborn, it will only be a matter of time until our seared consciences will capitulate on the life of the old, the infirm, the retarded, the handicapped, the different.

Biblical values demand a high view of life itself. Christians believe that we are the unique creation of God. We do not believe that life exists merely by impersonal chance. Rather, we believe that a personal God created us in His own image. This basic belief in the God-ordained dignity of human life ought to make every believer cry out against the crime of abortion.

In many ways abortion has been the first issue to surface that reveals the gradually changing attitudes of our society toward life itself. On January 22, 1973, the Supreme Court, in the *Roe v. Wade,* ruled that abortion on demand was a woman's legal right. In so doing the court invalidated previous national regulations against abortion.

In reaction to the decision John Noonan said: "By virtue of its (the court's) opinions, human life has less protection today than at any time since the inception of the country."[7] Watergate prosecutor Archibald Cox said that the court's ruling swept away "established law supported by the moral themes dominant in American life for more than a century."[8]

We live in a time of confused moral values, when people are more worried about baby seals than human babies. Interestingly, the same Supreme Court that legalized abortion also in 1973 halted the construction of the $116,000,000 Tellico Dam in Tennessee for fear it would wipe out a rare breed of fish!

Schaeffer and Koop also noted:

> The schizophrenic nature of our society became further evident as it became common practice for pediatricians to provide the maximum of resuscitative and supportive care in newborn intensive-care nurseries where premature infants were under their care—while obstetricians in the same medical centers were routinely destroying enormous numbers of unborn babies who were normal and frequently of larger size.[9]

We must oppose the choice to end the life of the unborn for our own selfish purposes. Every time I counsel a pregnant teenager, I encourage her to choose life for her baby. Even if she must also choose to let that child be adopted, she has given life to her child. I also applaud the efforts of those who are providing homes to care for pregnant women who have made the choice to let their babies live. We cannot condemn abortion without providing a better way for child care.[10]

## WHEN YOU THINK YOU'RE PREGNANT

I hope you will never have to read this section because of a personal crisis. But if you do, please pay careful attention. If you are pregnant, it is too late to reverse the process. The result of a promiscuous society is unplanned pregnancies out of wedlock. Please don't use this as an excuse to eliminate your baby. Remember, he or she is a real person too, deserving a chance at life just as much as you do.

Life began with God Himself. He passed it on to Adam and Eve, and they in turn passed it on to the human race. Whether you planned to get pregnant or not, you are now a part of that life-chain. You have given the gift of life to your baby. Don't take it away!

1. *See a doctor.* Get to a doctor as soon as possible for an examination to confirm the pregnancy. Don't run off and do anything foolish. Talk to the doctor openly and honestly.

2. *Tell your parents.* As tough as this will be, your parents need to know so they can help you through this decision. If you are afraid to go alone, take a pastor, youth worker, youth counselor, friend, or boyfriend with you. Don't wait. Do it right away.

3. *Don't overreact.* This is no time for panic; it is time for clear thinking and mature decisions. Running, screaming, or threatening suicide will not help matters. Don't argue with your parents. If they become angry, give them time to calm down. Remember, in a crisis we all tend to say things we later regret.

4. *Get spiritual guidance.* Go with your parents to see your pastor for spiritual advice. Don't be embarrassed. He is there to help. He may know of crisis pregnancy ministries of which you are unaware. The Liberty Godparent Homes of Lynchburg, Virginia, were started by Dr. Jerry Falwell and offer help for physical, emotional, and spiritual needs. You can contact them by calling 1-800-LIFE-AID.

5. *Confront the father.* If you know who got you pregnant and you have not yet confronted him, do so immediately. Take your parents or pastor with you if necessary. Don't let him blame the whole thing on you; he is responsible as well.

6. *Don't make any hasty decisions.* Just because you are pregnant you don't have to get married. In reality, marriage may be an impossibility right now. On the other hand, it may be ideal. Your pastor and parents will sense which option is best.

7. *Keep the baby alive.* Don't run to an abortion clinic. You will have to live with your decision for the rest of your life. Most women will tell you that, after it was too late, they deeply regretted getting an abortion. Choose to let the baby live. Then decide whether you will raise it or let someone else adopt it.

8. *Consider going to a ministry to unwed mothers.* Getting away may be the best thing for you right now. Christian

homes for pregnant girls exist all over the country. Call one and get some help there. You have lots of time before the baby comes to decide whether to keep it or put it up for adoption.

9. *Repent of your sin.* Don't forget that sin got you into this mess—don't go back to it! Turn your life over to Christ and let Him take control. Stop rationalizing about what happened, or how and why it happened. It's too late to dodge the facts. Accept your condition as it is for now.

10. *Rebuild your future.* You don't have to remain victimized. Shake off your past failures, confess your sin to God, and start to rebuild your future on a spiritual foundation. You can still be all He wants you to be. Don't give up or accept some secondary status because of what happened. You are God's child, washed in the blood of Jesus, and destined for eternal life.

## STARTING OVER

Rebuilding is tough for anyone to do, but it leads to a better life. Once you've decided whether to keep your baby or to have it adopted, you have to get on with your life.

Bobbie was a freshman in college when she got pregnant with twins by her boyfriend. At first he promised to marry her, but then he withdrew from school and went home. After several weeks it was obvious he wasn't coming back. She had to make a decision. She chose to keep the babies and raise them with her parents' help. Her father told the people at church what her situation was and they rallied in support of their family. About a year after the twins were born, Bobbie was married to a fine Christian young man who was glad to join this instant family.

Tammy was a senior in high school when she learned that she was pregnant after a date with a guy she hardly knew. She was emotionally broken and deeply remorseful over her sin. She chose to have the baby and give her up for adoption through a Christian agency that placed the child in a loving

Christian family. Tammy later went to college, met and married a fine Christian, and they eventually began a family of their own.

Both of these young women have scars—sin always leaves its mark on our lives. But in each case, the girls made a positive moral choice to keep their babies alive. They did not take the "easy" way out.

If you are rebuilding, consider the following suggestions:

1. *Don't give up.* It is too easy under pressure to give up on your decision to have the baby. Stick with your decision. In the long run you will be glad you did.

2. *Don't rationalize.* What has happened is now a reality. Don't try to rationalize it away. Face up to what led to the pregnancy, and determine not to let it happen again. Stop beating yourself emotionally with "what if's" because they don't change the facts.

3. *Decide what is best for the baby.* Don't make your decision to keep or adopt the baby to satisfy yourself. Instead, ask yourself what will really be best for this child in the long run. Then, once you have made your decision, stick to it.

4. *Give your baby the care it needs.* Even while you are pregnant, eat right, get exercise, and get plenty of sleep. Give the baby within you every possible consideration of care and nurture. If you choose to keep the child, give it all the love you can.

5. *Re-evaluate your life.* This is an excellent time to re-evaluate what your life is all about. What are you going to do in the future? How are you going to live? How should your behavior change after the pregnancy? Only you can answer these vital questions. Decide now that your life will count for God and for good in the future, and surrender to His will for your life.

## WHAT IF IT'S TOO LATE?

Jean was not a Christian when she got pregnant. She thought living the wild party life at school was the way to go. But at sixteen she got so drunk and stoned at a party that she lost all sense of control. Several guys had sex with her, and a few weeks later she realized that one of them had gotten her pregnant.

Bitter and confused, she went to an abortion clinic and had the baby aborted. Afterward, she tried to go on with her life, but it was never quite the same. Somehow she realized that there was too great a price to pay for loose living.

One day a friend invited Jean to one of our crusades. After several nights in attendance, she responded to the invitation to give her life to Christ.

"But I feel so dirty," she told the counselor. "I don't see how God could want me."

"If God waited for us to clean up ourselves," the counselor replied, "we would remain lost for sure."

"I want Him to forgive me," Jean said, "but I'm not sure I can live it."

"No one can live the Christian life without Christ," the counselor told her. "First, you have to let Him come in and take over."

"How do I do that?" Jean asked.

"By inviting Him to come into your life," the counselor replied. "The scripture says in Romans 10:13, "For whoever calls upon the name of the Lord shall be saved.""

"Does that apply to anyone—even me?" Jean asked.

"Yes it does," the counselor assured her.

Then the counselor, a college student from a nearby Christian school, looked at Jean and said, "I know why you're struggling, Jean."

"Why?" she questioned.

"Because I did the same thing myself four years ago. I thought my chances with God were shot. He'd never accept anyone like me. But He did, and He will forgive you too."

That night Jean confessed her sin and accepted by faith the cleansing that Christ offers us through His shed blood. She put her faith in His atoning death as the sufficient payment for her sin and left the service a newborn child of God.

Perhaps as you've read these accounts, you have said to

yourself, "It's too late for me. I've already made the wrong choice."

Let me assure you that it is never too late to come to Christ and start all over again. Nearly every story about Jesus in the gospels is a story of Him offering new life to someone. He forgave the woman taken in adultery (John 8). He offered a new beginning to the woman at the well who had been divorced five times (John 4). He gave spiritual insight to a legalistic old Pharisee (John 3). He called a despised tax collector to follow Him (Matthew 9). He restored Peter after he had denied Him (John 21).

Abortion is a tragic decision because it is a decision for death instead of life. It is a decision that cannot be reversed once it has been made. The decision to reject Christ is similar. It, too, is a decision for death instead of life. It, too, cannot be reversed once we pass from this life. If you have made a wrong decision with regard to abortion, please don't make another wrong decision with regard to Christ.

God does not condone our wrong and sinful behavior, but He does not leave us without hope either. Let Him cleanse your heart and heal your soul with His forgiving grace. The Bible promises, "For God did not send His Son into the world to condemn the world, but that the world through Him might be saved" (John 3:17).

God's love is so great that it can overcome life's greatest mistakes and heal life's greatest hurts. If you are searching for love, joy, and peace, search no more. He is all that you want and all you will ever need. Trust Him today.

## Chapter 12

# Why Do
# Christians
# Fail?

WHETHER WE UNDERSTAND it or not, Christians fail too. Some have read these accounts of men and women who turned from a life of doubt to one of faith and asked, "But what happens to professing Christians who fail?" Most of us can understand why nonbelievers feel trapped by their past, but what about believers?

Tom grew up in an outstanding church in Florida, and had been a professing Christian since he was a young teenager. He was active in the youth groups, and as a college student, he took an active role in the church's singles ministry. But halfway through college, he began to burn out. Caught between the pressures of study and ministry, he lost his zeal for Christ. Eventually, he began dating an unbeliever. They fell in love and soon became careless in their behavior.

"I couldn't seem to help myself," Tom said when we met one morning for breakfast. "I fell for her like a ton of bricks!"

"How long did you see each other?" I asked, trying to eat my eggs and listen at the same time.

"About two years," he replied. "Our relationship got out of control and she got pregnant. We still saw each other regularly after that and I just assumed we would get married."

Tom's face dropped and his expression turned sour as he explained what happened.

"Then, one day she said, 'I just can't have this baby. I've got too many things I still want to do with my life.'

"I asked what she meant, and she told me she was going to have an abortion. She was so casual about it. I tried to object, but she had already made the appointment.

"Despite my pleas," he said, "she went ahead with the abortion. Not long after that we broke up and she moved to New York to take a job."

The distress and agony on his face was overwhelming. I dropped my fork and reached out to touch his shoulder as he began to cry.

"Jay, I never wanted something like this," he sobbed. "I feel like I've failed God."

"You have," I replied gently, "but He hasn't failed you. It's never too late to turn back."

I reminded him of all the recorded "failures" in the Bible. Adam condemned the entire human race, yet he was the first person to receive God's grace. Abraham was guilty of lying, adultery, and laughing at God, yet he is remembered as the father of the faithful. Moses never made it to the promised land, yet he was one of Israel's greatest leaders. Aaron succumbed to idolatry, yet he became God's high priest. Samson fell to Delilah, yet he was Israel's greatest warrior. David committed adultery and murder, yet he was Israel's greatest king. Peter denied the Lord, yet he was God's spokesman at Pentecost.

We shouldn't, and we certainly don't have to, but we do often fail. To fail is to be human. But to deal with failure is divine. God's great grace forgives our failures and sets us back on course again.

"Jay, what should I do?" Tom asked.

"Well, you certainly have a heavy cross to bear," I reminded him. "But it's still possible to turn your life in the right direction."

"How?" he asked.

"First," I replied, "you are going to have to settle this matter with God. You have denied Him and, like Peter, you are going to have to reaffirm your love for Him. Secondly, you ought to seek that woman's forgiveness for the wrong you did to her, even though she may have encouraged it. You failed to be the kind of witness and example to her that you should have been. Then, you need to begin to rebuild your life and testimony. You need to get back into church and publicly rededicate your life to Christ."

As we continued to talk together, we discussed Tom's spiritual pilgrimage. He had wandered far off the trail and needed to get out of the canyon of self-pity and back on the road again. I suggested that he work with the singles pastor at his church in order to establish a basis for his discipleship and accountability.

In the months that followed his life began to turn around. The joy of his relationship to Christ returned. And though many of the steps he had to take were difficult, he soon returned to useful service to the Lord. In time, he married a committed Christian girl who forgave him of the past and built a relationship with him based upon Christ.

## FAILURE IS NOT THE END!

The key to overcoming failure is to recognize that it can be overcome. Although we all fail in one way or another, we shouldn't simply excuse ourselves for being less than we should be. But we can rejoice that we are not alone in our struggles. In his helpful book *Another Chance,* Dean Merrill wrote:

I believe in the God of the second chance. I believe in the God who is not put off by our fiascos . . . who has an uncanny ability to bring good out of disaster . . . His mercy . . . endures for the person who has made an undeniable mistake in his life, whose future has been torpedoed by one or more fateful acts. The person who has stepped outside of his marriage . . . the trusted employee who has mishandled corporate funds . . . the woman who has borne an illegitimate child . . . the man who has rejected his early faith and turned instead to drugs or alcohol . . . the person who has betrayed his family.[1]

As Merrill pointed out, the mercy of God endures all human failure. When our dreams have been smashed, our hopes dashed, and our future has gone blank, God is still there. He never gives up on His children. That is why, in spite of our failures, we always come running back to Him. We cannot turn our back on Him because we are His children. The apostle Paul understood this when he wrote, "We are hard pressed on every side, yet not crushed; we are perplexed, but not in despair; persecuted, but not forsaken; struck down, but not destroyed . . . that the life of Jesus also may be manifested in our mortal flesh" (2 Corinthians 4:8, 9, 11). Even when all else has gone wrong, Jesus is still at work within us to make us more like Himself.

In his classic work *Failure: The Back Door to Success,* Erwin Lutzer wrote, "To talk about the 'ideal' life is quite futile. . . . The only ideal life will be in heaven, and if you are reading this, you're not there!"[2]

Life on earth often falls short of the ideal God has set for us. But He does not give up on us just because we have given up on Him. He keeps pursuing us until we are in complete submission to Him and His will for our lives.

Somebody once said: Justice means we get what we deserve, whereas mercy means we do not get what we deserve. Beyond this is grace, by which we get what we do not deserve. That is how great God's plan is for our lives. We not only miss the punishment we deserve, but we are granted His righteousness, which we could never deserve.

In their book *When the Road Gets Rough,* Ed Hindson and Walt Byrd give four points for dealing with failure:[3]

1. *To fail is to be human.* God is fully aware of our weaknesses and limitations. While He is not the author of our mistakes, He can and does overrule them for our own good. The psalmist put it this way: "For He knows our frame; He remembers that we are dust" (Psalm 103:14). God fully understands our limitations and how to use us despite them. He can work around the obstacles in our lives to bring about His perfect will.

2. *To fail is not to be a failure.* One failure does not mean

you are destined to a life of failure. Even the most successful people fail at times. For example, Babe Ruth not only set a baseball record for home runs, but he also set a record for strike-outs in the same season. Based on his success as a player, no one would call Babe Ruth a failure. He overcame his weaknesses by his strengths. For the Christian, God overcomes our weaknesses by His strength.

3. *No one is a failure until he stops trying.* We never learn the limits of our ability or vulnerability until we reach the point of total failure. Thus, it is better to attempt much and occasionally fail than to attempt nothing and achieve it. Thomas Edison tried over five thousand different types of light-bulb filaments without success before finding one that worked. His persistence gave us the modern electric light. In the same manner, believers need to keep on pursuing their walk with God. Your stumbling does not mean that it is time to give up the race.

4. *Failure is never final as long as we get up one more time than we fall down.* If you have fallen, get up again and keep going. Fear is as crippling as failure. Some people never get back in the race because they are afraid to fail again. If you have failed, admit it and start over. Accept God's forgiveness as an accomplished fact in your life. Don't let your past dominate your present and frustrate your future. Focus on your goals, not your failures. Move ahead with God's guidance, for nothing worthwhile was ever accomplished without some risk. You may face certain limitations, but God has not saved you and gifted you with certain abilities so you could just sit there wallowing in your failure. Get up and get going again.

It is also important to stop making excuses for your mistakes. That only tells people that you are still struggling. When you can put the problem behind you, you won't have to keep talking about it. If it is resolved and settled, then leave it that way and move on to a better life.

When people refuse to face their failure honestly, they never solve the problems that led to it in the first place. As a result, their situation never turns around and they remain stuck in the mire of self-pity. In reality God wants us to deal with our failures in such a way that He can erase them and we can go on to success in serving Him.

## PICKING UP THE PIECES

I am convinced that Christians fail because they become blinded by the glitter of sin. Those who have experienced the degradation of sin can see past the glitter because of their personal experience with the consequences of sin. But those who have been raised in church, who made an early profession of faith, and who have been sheltered from the horror of sin, often find it attractive in later years.

Marlene was such a person. She had committed her life to Christ when she was ten years old. During her teenage years she was active in her church youth group and had an outstanding Christian testimony at her home church. After graduation she decided to attend her state university.

"I can handle a secular school if I live at home," she had told herself. But the prevalence of sin and the pressure to conform was far greater than she ever imagined. At first she regularly attended meetings at the Baptist Student Union on campus, but as she began to drift away from the Lord, she stopped attending.

"I remember the night I went over the edge," she told me. We were talking together after I had shared my testimony with the students at her university's Baptist Student Union. I had told them how I had messed up my life and how Christ had changed me.

"I went to see an R-rated movie with some girlfriends. I thought I was mature enough to handle it. Afterward, some guys met us and offered us some marijuana. The other girls accepted and began to pressure me to take it too. I felt so awkward, I wanted to run. But I knew I couldn't, so I took it and smoked a few puffs, just to prove I could handle it.

"The whole bunch of us got high," she continued, "and the girls all got silly. Then the guys talked us into coming over to their apartment for another round. Before the night was over, I was totally stoned and had had sex with two of them. When I woke up the next morning, I was lying on the floor, undressed, and everyone else was already up.

"I asked one of the girls where everyone was, and she casually replied that the guys had had to go and told us to lock the door when we left.

"I remember," Marlene said, "sitting there, slumped over, thinking I had given myself and my virginity away to a couple of guys I didn't even know and who didn't even have the decency to say good-bye. I was so down on myself for what I'd done that I thought, What does it matter now? I lost all sense of control and self-respect, and before long I was partying constantly and going all the way with just about anybody who came along.

"I tried to tell myself that God didn't even exist so it didn't matter how I lived. I was trying to buy all the humanism I was hearing in class because I didn't want to face myself."

After more than a year, Marlene had come to her senses and realized she was destroying her life. "A friend told me you were speaking at the BSU and invited me to come. When I walked through the door, I realized I had not been here in a long time and I'm not the same person who was here before."

I could see the pain on Marlene's face and sense the agony in her voice. She paused several minutes, then looked at me and asked, "Jay, how can God ever forgive me? I'm a Christian and I know better."

"Marlene," I responded, "being a Christian doesn't automatically exempt you from making mistakes. It is true that you ought to know better, but that doesn't change the fact of what has happened. God's forgiveness is just as much available to you as it was to me."

"Are you sure God will forgive me?" she asked with concern on her face.

"Yes, I am," I replied confidently. "The verse in the Bible that says, 'If we confess our sins, He is faithful and just to forgive us our sins' (1 John 1:9) is for believers. God can and will forgive you when you repent of your sin, confess it to Him and turn away from it."

"I really want to come back to the Lord," Marlene said. "Can you pray with me?"

"Sure, let's do it right now."

As we bowed our heads together, Marlene poured out her heart to God. She expressed brokenhearted sorrow over her sinful attitudes and behavior. She acknowledged that what had happened was her fault and asked God to cleanse her and give her the strength to live for Him.

A few years later I learned that she had graduated, married a committed Christian, and they were living for Christ and serving Him in their local church.

Rob had a similar story. He had trusted the Lord as a teenager at a youth camp. But two years later, during his senior year in high school, he got drunk on a class trip. It was his first experience with alcohol, and it left him smashed.

During the rest of his senior year, Rob kept drinking, just to be one of the gang. And as time went on, his drinking got totally out of control. By June after his graduation, he was ticketed for drunk driving, and in August he had an accident while driving drunk.

"My parents really threw a fit," he told me when we first talked about it. "They have always been strong church people and just couldn't understand how I could get this way."

"How *did* you get this way, Rob?" I asked him.

"By trying to get everyone to like me," he said. "I know it sounds bad, but I just got tired of always being made fun of for being a good kid."

"How do you feel now?" I asked.

"Pretty lousy."

"Then it really hasn't worked, has it?" I asked.

"No, it sure hasn't, Jay," he answered. "What's the matter with me?"

"The same thing as every Christian who turns his back on what he knows to be right," I said. "You were blinded by the glitter!"

"What do you mean?" Rob asked.

"I mean that you were enticed by the fun part of sin," I said. "It glitters and sparkles until you become entrapped by it. Then it turns sour and ugly. What seemed so wonderful ends up becoming something terrible that can ruin your life.

"Are you at a point where you are ready to turn away from this?" I asked.

"Yes," he said, "I've had enough."

After we talked together for a while, and then prayed, I reminded Rob that alcohol has a powerful physical pull on people. I warned him that once he cleaned out his system there could be withdrawals and even a few months later he could hit the wall—just as I had done so long ago.

"If you can still say no to it then," I added, "you will be able to defeat it."

Rob made it, and today he is attending a Christian college and studying to be an attorney. Unfortunately, there are many kids like Rob who don't make it. They make a profession of faith in Christ during their childhood, but fall away from the Lord in their teenage years. Some get so far away they never come back.

## THE ROAD BACK

The road of life is paved with good intentions that never become reality. If you are away from God, the time to start back is now. In his helpful book *Starting Over,* Charles Swindoll says, "To start over, you have to know where you are."[4] You can't find direction for the road ahead if you don't know where you are now.

It is time to take stock of yourself. Close down for inventory for a minute. Ask yourself, If I keep living the way I am, where will I end up? Be honest, and, if necessary, be tough on yourself. Admit your failure and confess your need for God's forgiveness. Openly declare that you need Him, and freely accept His grace and help.

When we want to give up, God bestows more grace than

we ever could have imagined. When we say, "No way!" He says, "I am the Way." When we say, "No chance!" He says, "I'll give you another chance." When we say, "No hope!" He says, "I am your hope."

Trusting God to forgive us, as believers, may be as difficult as trusting Him the first time we believed He was our Savior. That's because we are so full of pride, we hate to admit we've failed. We believe we are supposed to have the answers—we are supposed to know better. And we are! We need to apply the answers we already know. But we will fail, so we need to get back in the race and remember that we will make it by the grace of God. God loves us so much that He is willing to save us from our sins not only the first time we come to Him by faith, but also every time we come to Him.

Perhaps you have been away from God for a period of time. You once knew Him and loved Him, but now you hardly ever acknowledge that He is there. You have been living for yourself and you've pushed God into the back seat of your life.

Now is the time to turn your life over to Him afresh. As long as you've got breath, you have an opportunity to make things right with God. Don't go on through life running from the God who loves you. He wants to reconcile you to Himself.

Whenever we believers fail, the world loves to mock and scorn. But when a broken believer recommits his life to Christ, his testimony can be regained. It is never too late to come back to Christ.

When I look back on my teenage years, I see that God has used my mistakes to help me minister to others. I know people's excuses and I know the pain they are in. But when I see Christians fail, it breaks my heart because I know they are in for a rough ride. If they really know Christ, they can never be satisfied with a life of rebellion against Him.

Too many times Christians are blinded by the glitter of sin. They think they are missing out on something by not sinning and wonder, "Maybe this is better than what I've been told." But, like Adam and Eve biting the fruit, they are in for a rude awakening.

Sin never satisfies. Sin thrills, but then it kills. It looks great until you have to look at it every day. It feels good until it has control of your body, and then it slowly chokes you to death.

If I could leave any positive appeal with professing Christians, it would be to live for Christ and enjoy your life with Him. Don't be fooled into thinking you're missing out on something. What you are missing out on is a headache, a hangover, venereal disease, terminal illness. Whenever you decide to live for God, you will be the winner, not the loser.

My friend, if you are away from the Lord, He is out looking for you. Just like the shepherd looks for a lost sheep until he finds it, in spite of the circumstances, God looks for you. Whether you love Him or not, whether you deserve His love or not, whether your sin is the smallest or the greatest, He cares for you and will never stop calling your name until He finds you, the one for whom He gave His life on Calvary. You can come home to peace, forgiveness, a new start. He'll even give you the faith to trust Him if only you ask.

If you've already experienced this forgiveness and you know someone else who has recently turned back to God, encourage them along the way. If they stumble, help them get up. If they need to talk, listen. If they need advice, give it. Promise to pray and be available to them.

It is so easy for us to condemn people when they are down, and then neglect them when they try to get up. Remember the apostle Paul's attitude about John Mark? Paul himself had been a rogue and scoundrel. He had hunted, hounded, and murdered Christians. When he was converted to Christ, several believers doubted his sincerity. They were reluctant to trust him, but Barnabas spoke up and defended him. Later he and Barnabas took Mark on one of their missionary journeys. When the going got tough, Mark went home. On the next journey Barnabas wanted to forgive Mark and take him along, but Paul would have nothing to do with him. How quickly we forget!

You were not always a shining light, a glowing example, a pillar of the church. There was a time when God had to meet you where you were at the point of your need. When He did, you were thrilled with His grace and threw yourself by faith upon His love.

When a fellow believer stumbles, be the first, not the last, to welcome him back with open arms. Let him know you've missed him and are glad he has come home. Don't be self-righteous like the prodigal's elder brother. When people have failed, they have already suffered, and they've probably already learned their lesson. That's why they are back, looking for love, forgiveness, and acceptance.


## NO SCAR?

Hast thou no scar?
No hidden scar on foot, or side, or hand?
I hear thee sung as mighty in the land,
I hear them hail thy bright ascendant star,
Hast thou no scar?
Hast thou no wound?
Yet I was wounded by the archers, spent,
Leaned Me against a tree to die; and rent
By ravening beasts that compassed Me,
I swooned:
Hast thou no wound?
No wound, no scar?
Yet, as the Master shall the servant be,
And, pierced are the feet that follow Me;
But thine are whole: can he have followed far
Who has no wound nor scar?

*by Amy Carmichael*

# HOPE
# FOR
# THE
# FUTURE

## Chapter 13

# Can God
# Ever
# Forgive Me?

THE EASTERN AIRLINES jet broke through the dreary, rainy clouds on its approach to the Orlando runway. As the pilot banked slightly to the left and we began our landing, I could see the city faintly below.

I had flown all night from Albuquerque, New Mexico, to visit a woman who was dying of cancer at Orange Memorial Hospital. She was a special lady, and I wanted to see her before she passed away.

As we disembarked from the plane I could feel the warm, damp Florida air outside. I walked to the baggage area, picked up my suitcase, and walked over to the car rental. While I was filling out the forms to rent the car, I kept thinking about the woman I was going to see, wondering what it must be like to face death. *It must be a hopeless feeling,* I thought to myself. *I wonder if she is really ready to meet God?*

I felt compelled to speak to the woman face to face, before it was too late. She had demonstrated a great deal of love for me in the past, but never seemed to be able to articulate her own faith clearly.

The drive across town passed quickly as I thought about what I would say to her when I arrived. When I pulled into the hospital parking lot and got out of the car, the rain was coming down like a curtain of fine mist.

As I walked down the corridor to the south wing, her doctor met me. "She has cancer of the colon," the doctor began to explain, "and it's inoperable at this stage. She only has a few months to live."

"Does she know this?" I inquired.

"Yes, she does," the doctor replied abruptly. "And she's quite concerned. I guess that's why you're here."

"Well, I want to do anything I can to help," I said.

Walking down the corridor, I heard an announcement for a Mr. Strack to report to the front desk. As I responded to the page, I was informed that the call was for Gary Strack, the administrator of the hospital.

As I turned to walk away, someone called out "Jay!" A tall, lean man I had never seen before approached. "You don't know me," he said, "but I've wanted to meet you for some time. They paged me because I am the C.E.O. (Chief Executive Officer) of this hospital. I am also your brother."

I stared at him for a few minutes before I could speak. "Are you sure about this?"

"Yes," he said smiling. "We have the same father, but different mothers."

Gary went on to explain that my father had been married before he met my mother and had a son by that marriage, but I had never been told.

"I know it's hard to believe," Gary said, "but it's true."

As I looked at him, I realized that he was tall, like my Dad, and had many of the same features. He knew many facts about my father, and we talked for a few minutes in what I admit was an awkward experience. We were both trying to reach out across the barriers of time to each other.

"You know Dad is doing much better now," he explained. "He is active in Alcoholics Anonymous as a speaker and lecturer. He even ran a successful place called the Bowling Green Inn in Bowling Green, Florida."

As we talked we shared the hurt and pain we had experienced as teenagers because of what alcohol had done in Dad's life. "That's all changed now," Gary said. "He's really a different man."

After a few more moments of conversation, Gary suggested that I get to my appointment. As we shook hands, we both seemed to sense the bond between us. We exchanged addresses and phone numbers and promised to stay in touch.

Excited but bewildered, I walked down the corridor. *How could I have a brother I never met?* I thought. *Our family sure was a mess!*

When I reached the room where the woman I came to visit was, I stopped outside to catch my breath. *What should I say to her?* I wondered. Then, remembering that her own faith seemed unclear, I knew what I had to say.

I knocked gently on the door, and a feeble voice replied, "Come in." The room was dark and gloomy. The shades had been pulled down and the curtains drawn shut. As I peered through the darkness, I noticed her silver-gray hair glistening and shining from the hallway light. She seemed much older and grayer than her years. She had lived a tough life, and it had taken its toll on her.

"I came as soon as I could," I said, explaining that I had flown all night from out West.

"I'm just glad you're here, Jay," she said weakly. "I need to talk to you."

I asked her if she knew the seriousness of her condition, and she acknowledged that she did. Then I asked her if she was ready to meet God, and she said that she was not.

"I know I have prayed before," she said, "but my relationship with God is not good enough to die with."

I tried to explain to her that God loved her and wanted to save her.

"But you don't understand," she said. "I've made so many mistakes."

"Now wait a minute," I interrupted. "Your going to heaven doesn't depend on how good you've been. It only depends on the fact that Christ died for your sins. He took all your mistakes on Himself and put them to death for you."

As we continued talking, I kept quoting Isaiah 1:18, " *'Come now, and let us reason together,' says the Lord, 'Though your sins are like scarlet, They shall be as white as snow; Though they are red like crimson, They shall be as wool.'* "

"Listen to that promise," I insisted. "God meant this for you just as much as He meant it for me or for anyone."

"But what about all my failures?" she insisted.

"If God can't forgive you, then He certainly won't forgive me," I replied. "Look at all the wrongs I've done. Yet, He has forgiven me because I asked Him to and believed that He would."

"But can He ever forgive someone like me?" she asked.

"Yes, Mom," I said soberly, "I know He can forgive you."

In the moments that followed, I watched my mother pray and claim God's cleansing, forgiveness, and salvation. She poured her heart out to God as genuinely and sincerely as I have ever heard anyone pray.

In the weeks that followed, she was a different person. She expressed joy and peace in her relationship to God. There was a smile on her face and an inner beauty that radiated within her. In the months she had left, she became a dynamic witness for Christ.

I cannot tell you the joy that I experienced in leading my own mother to Christ. I reassured her many times in those months of my love for her. I also explained that many of my earlier problems were my own fault, not hers. I also reminded her of what God had done for me in turning my life around to His glory.

I had seen thousands of people come to Christ in my crusade meetings. But seeing my own mother accept Christ was the greatest thrill of my ministry.

She went to be with the Lord in 1980, and though I miss her, I know she is in heaven with our Lord—a far better place than she ever knew here below. I have experienced guilt over what kind of son I was. My crusade schedule often prevented me from being with her as I wanted to be. But I am grateful for my other half brother, Rocky, who was able to be with her almost constantly and who was a great source of comfort to her when she needed it.

As the years have passed, my father and I have been able to

communicate about the scars of the past. I better understand the pain and agony he was in because of alcohol. It has also been a thrill to watch him change his life, and, as a result, help hundreds of others who are struggling with the same problems. Dad has been actively involved in helping alcoholics through the years. He remembers all too clearly the pain that alcohol brought into our lives and is committed to seeing others delivered from its curse.

God has done a great work in our family. Most of us have been reunited in fellowship and harmony with one another. We all have reasons to rejoice now, despite the pain of the past.

Don't let hurts in your background prevent the joy of restored relationships. You may say it doesn't make up for the hurt of the past, but it sure does help the hurt of today and offer joy for tomorrow.

That is what my ministry is all about. It is a ministry to hurting people whose lives are racked by sin and who are looking for help. There is always a way out if you will take it. God invaded our lives, gave us hope, and turned us around. I believe He can do the same thing for you.

God loved us so much that He sent His Son, Jesus Christ, to die on the cross for our sins. He did not die merely as a victim of some plot or as a martyr to some cause. He died as a substitute in our place. All the wrath of God against our sin was poured out on Him on the cross. And when He died, He died for us.

In place of the death and judgment we deserve, God offers us eternal life in Christ. We can live forever because our lives have become transformed by Him.

## TIME FOR A DECISION

There are crucial junctures in our lives when we must make important decisions that affect our futures. Perhaps you are at one of those junctures now. You know that you cannot go on as you have been going. Something has to change and that something is you.

The Old Testament records the account of the children of

Israel's fleeing from Egypt (Exodus 14). They had been in bondage for four hundred years and longed for a deliverer. But when Moses led them out, they were fearful and afraid. They finally made their way to the edge of the Red Sea, where they were trapped between Pharaoh's pursuing army and the waters of the sea. At that point they had only three options: 1) go back; 2) stand still; 3) go forward.

The same is true for each of us. If we really want to be free from the bondage of the world, we must break from it completely and move ahead. Once we have been truly converted we know we can't go back. We don't belong there any more, and we'll never be comfortable if we try to go back.

I remember the struggle in my own life shortly after my conversion. I knew what I had to do to go forward for God. But Satan threw everything he had at me to keep me down. At times I was tempted to go back to my old life, but I knew I could never be happy with it again. As I sat on the beach that day and wrote my sins in the sand and watched the waves wash them away, I knew I could never go back.

Perhaps you realize that you can't go back to your old life, but you have become stuck where you are now. You are standing still, waiting for direction from God. Sometimes we need to do that. We need to stop right where we are, take stock of ourselves, and seek a fresh direction from God.

Moses told the Israelites to "stand still" for a brief moment. But then the Lord parted the waters and told them to go forward.

You can't remain stalled in indecision all your life. If you have been stalled at the standing still phase, it's time to face the future and move ahead. Seek God's direction for your life. Make whatever decisions and commitments are necessary and move on.

Finally, there is the move-ahead phase. God told the Israelites to cross the parted Red Sea. This brought a whole new dimension into their lives as they began to learn to walk by faith. That is what you may need to do. Stop analyzing your options and step out by faith.

If you have failed in some area of your life, confess it to God, turn away from it, and follow the Lord. He wants you to surrender to His will and purpose for your life. So do it! Stop making excuses, and put your decisions into action. You may be at the greatest crossroads of your life. God is there! Trust Him to lead you in your decision. Make the decision, and make it work to the glory of God.

I have watched thousands of people come to that point of decision. Some come and embrace Christ by faith; others hesitate; and some reject. Don't be like those latter two groups. Come to Him by faith now. Bring all your burdens and heartaches, because He will care for them. Let Him transform you into a testimony of His grace.

Never think that you are not good enough for Him. None of us are good enough in ourselves. But He loves us in spite of what we are. He delights to take us and make us into what we are not. Without Him, we are nothing. But with Him, we are everything we need to be in life.

Today is the day for you to get out of the valley of decision. With your past forgiven, the power of God in your life for today, and the promise of Heaven tomorrow, the best is yet to come for you. *Shake off the dust* of the past, and get on with the rest of your life.

# Chapter 14 ◄

# It's Never
# Too
# Late!

DRIVING ON THE Los Angeles freeway is one of the most awesome things a Florida boy can tackle. Thousands of cars dart at incredible speeds across six to eight lanes of traffic with an indifference that is inconceivable to an outsider. I merely try to survive the whole ordeal as though it were a NASCAR race.

We were driving toward Pomona one day, talking about our upcoming crusade, when my host asked me if I were ever tempted to go back to my old lifestyle.

"Well," I said, rather surprised, "I suppose we are all tempted by things at times. But I spent too long in the far country, and I can still taste the slop!"

I was referring to the imagery in Jesus' parable of the prodigal son in Luke 15:11–32. It is the story of a wealthy man who had two sons. One of the sons insisted he be given his share of the inheritance, left home, and went to a far country, where he wasted all of his wealth on riotous living. He fell so low that he ended up eating slop with the pigs before he finally came to repentance and returned to his father. When he did return, the son begged his father to forgive him and let him work as one of his hired servants. Instead, his father was so glad to see him, that he ordered his best robe to clothe him and put a ring on his finger and shoes on his feet. Then he ordered a banquet and fully reinstated him.

Every time I read that story, my heart rejoices. I am reminded afresh that my heavenly Father loves to forgive us and take us back. Perhaps you have read the accounts in this book and said to yourself, "But my situation is different. You don't know what I have done."

It doesn't matter what you have done. God's grace is greater than all of your sin. His love is deeper than all of your rebellion. His mercy is wider than all of your failure. He can do for you what you cannot do for yourself. He can cleanse, pardon, and forgive you. He can give you a brand new life and a brand new start in life.

The other thing I always remember about this story is the contrast between the slop of the hogpen and the banquet of the father. Too many times we forget how deceptive the illusions of the world really are. The devil wants us to think we are missing out on something wonderful when, in reality, we are missing out on something hideous. Don't be blinded by the glitter of this world. Underneath the facade of the good times are brokenhearted people crying out for love and forgiveness.

Every time I walk into a youth hang-out and smell the marijuana in the air, my heart aches for kids who are looking for life in all the wrong places. I know because I've been there. It is an empty and hollow existence covered over by cheap tinsel to make it look good.

## THINGS AREN'T ALWAYS AS THEY SEEM

Paul was a handsome high-school junior. He had blond hair and stood over six-feet tall. The girls loved him and the guys envied him. He had it all—looks, grades, and sports. He was quarterback for the football team and star pitcher for the baseball team. And he was an honor student.

Everybody assumed Paul had it all together. But inside he was a restless young man, struggling with his very existence. During times of depression, he began taking uppers to keep himself going.

"Once you're a winner," he told me, "you feel like you have

to keep winning to be accepted. When I first started playing sports, they were fun games. But now they are a big pressure in my life."

That pressure got so great that Paul cracked during his junior year. He overdosed on drugs in a deliberate attempt to commit suicide. Fortunately, his parents discovered him in the backyard just in time to rush him to the hospital.

"They weren't supposed to be home," he said later. "I never dreamed I'd still be alive."

His parents called me the morning he was rushed to the hospital, and I immediately went to see him. He was still pretty groggy when we began to talk, but he eventually came out of the fog.

"I'm sorry, Jay," he said. "I really blew it. I just couldn't handle it anymore."

"You should have opened up and asked for help," I said.

"I kept telling myself I could handle it. But now I realize I was only fooling myself." Then Paul looked at me and asked, "How can I ever go back and face people at church or school? I feel so ridiculous and foolish. My testimony is shot."

"It may be tarnished," I said, "but it's never totally shot as long as you're alive and can turn it around."

"You don't understand," he replied, "it's too late for that."

"No it's not," I answered. "It's never too late to do what is right!"

Although it took some stern talk, Paul finally began to realize the truth I was trying to drive home to him: It is never too late to turn around. I don't care how old or young you are, God can still work in your heart.

## SHAKE OFF THE DUST

Far too many of us never find what God has for us in life because we are trapped by our past sins and failures. I want to urge you to shake off the dust of the past. As long as you remain a prisoner of the past, you will never know the freedom of the future. Only when you rise above your circumstances and failures can you truly begin to rebuild a better life.

You can't spend the rest of your life sitting in the ashes of devastation, crying over what went wrong. All the remorse in the world won't change anything. True, there is a time to mourn and cry, but there is also a time to rejoice again.

When you come to the end of yourself and discover that Christ is all there is, you will also discover that He is all you need! When you make that discovery, Jesus Christ will be so evident in your life that others will see His character instead of your old character.

If you are still struggling with your past, consider these important points.

1. *The past is past.* You cannot go back and relive the past. No matter how much you wish you could, you cannot undo the wrongs that were done. But you can change the present, and that will change the future. Stop beating yourself with the club of the past. Bury it and move on.

2. *Stop making excuses.* Some people never shake off their pasts because they continue making excuses for what went wrong. They think the excuses will lessen their guilt, but instead, the guilt increases because they are keeping the issue alive. Stop thinking and talking about it.

3. *Turn it over to God.* Once you have really turned the whole matter over to God, you don't have to keep worrying about it. If He has forgiven you, the matter is settled. Leave it settled, and go on with the rest of your life. Digging it up again only says that you really haven't given it to God and left it with Him.

4. *Seek His will for the future.* The important thing in your life now is to find God's leading for your future. What does He want to do through you now? His will for your life may well include using your testimony to benefit others who are struggling with the same problems.

5. *Rebuild your life and testimony.* No matter how much time it takes, rebuilding is always worth the effort. Don't be

afraid to start over. Clear your conscience with those you have wronged and then get involved in an active church where the fellowship will encourage you and the body of believers will hold you accountable for your growth and progress.

6. *Don't try to go it alone.* It's tough enough to make it with help and encouragement; don't try to do it all by yourself. The pressure will get to you. Let others share your burdens and help you through the tough times. Together you will form closer friendships and build a better future.

7. *Don't give up.* Even when the rebuilding is tough, remember, it's better than the way things were when they were in a mess. Don't crack under the load. God will see you through, and one day you will be able to look back on this as a positive, character-building time in your life.

8. *Establish positive goals.* While you are rebuilding, set positive goals of spiritual progress for yourself. Pray, read, study, meditate, and memorize. Build up the weak areas in your life. Just as an athlete builds up his physical body, so you must build up your spiritual life and reinforce the weak areas.

9. *Stay away from temptation.* Don't go back to whatever or whoever dragged you down in the first place. You can't defeat alcohol by hanging around in a bar. Neither can you overcome any temptation while making yourself vulnerable to it. Get away from it and stay away from it.

10. *Let Christ be magnified.* Don't try to prove that you have changed. That won't impress anybody. Let people see Christ magnified in your life, and they will be impressed by Him. When He gets the glory, we have to stand in the background where we belong. When that happens, even your critics will rejoice with you because of God's victory in your life.

## REPENTANCE, REBUILDING, AND RESTORATION

One of the most beautiful restorations I have ever witnessed involved a dynamic couple named Ted and Sharon. They were outstanding Christians with vibrant testimonies.

Ted was a contracter and Sharon was an executive secretary for a major corporation. Both were also active at church—Ted, a deacon, and Sharon, the church organist. In addition, they had three lovely children. Their whole family was a perfect picture of success—on the outside.

Inwardly, their marriage left a lot to be desired. Ted was an aggressive businessman, a workaholic who spent long hours on the job making sure his company was the best. Sharon was also very involved in her job, but she craved attention and affection, which Ted was too busy to provide. Through the years, they steadily grew apart. Each found happiness and fulfillment in his or her work instead of in each other.

Eventually Sharon became romantically involved with her employer. It started off innocently enough—a few late nights, coffee, dinner, the companionship of working together on projects. Soon their lust for each other was out of control. She began making excuses for the long hours and late nights and even a few weekend business trips. But Ted was so busy, he never even noticed.

"I want a divorce," Sharon demanded late one evening after the kids were in bed.

"For what?" asked Ted, completely bewildered and unprepared for her announcement.

"For years of neglect, that's what!" Sharon shouted.

"You've got to be kidding!" Ted responded. "You've got everything anybody could ever want."

"That's not true," barked Sharon. "I don't have love and I don't have you."

After a long argument and ensuing discussion, Sharon finally admitted she had been seeing her employer, was in love, and wanted a divorce. Ted could hardly believe what he was hearing. At first he tried to defend himself and blame the whole affair on Sharon. Then he calmed down and said, "No, it's my fault. I have been working too hard. I have neglected you and the kids. I don't blame you for wanting to leave."

Sharon seemed reassured to hear this admission that had

been so long in coming. Then Ted appealed to her, "Please don't leave me. Give us a chance to work it out." Reluctantly, Sharon agreed.

The next day she broke off her relationship with her boss. That night Ted and Sharon came to one of our crusade services, hoping to find some answers. I preached on the theme of forgiveness, and their hearts began to melt as they sat, holding hands, tears running down their cheeks. During the invitation they both came forward to recommit their lives and their marriage to Christ.

After the service they explained to me why they had come. They were standing arm-in-arm, knowing they had nearly lost each other.

"What should we do now?" they asked.

"If no one else knows about this," I suggested, "then you need to settle it with God and each other. You need to forgive each other and start to rebuild your marriage."

They nodded their heads in agreement. Then I said, "Sharon, you need to resign from your job and get away from that other man. You can't stay there, even with the best of intentions, and make it work. Besides, you don't really need the money as much as you need each other."

Then I suggested they immediately get away on a honeymoon. The change of scenery would help them forget their hurts and focus on their rebuilding process.

In the months that followed their marriage took a dramatic turn for the better. They began praying together daily and spending quality time together. Even their children noticed the difference and commented on it. Ted and Sharon's marriage was saved because they took time to correct their problems and rearrange their priorities. For them it was not too late.

I believe it is not too late for millions of others too, if they will simply turn to Christ for help. As Paul said, "One thing I do, forgetting those things which are behind and reaching forward to those things which are ahead" (Philippians 3:13).

Whatever the dust of your life may be, the time has come to shake it off. It is time to come to grips with your past, deal with it, and turn away from it. You no longer need to be the prisoner of your past. God is in the business of graciously forgiving our sins and burying our past. The road of life is long and difficult. There are many potholes and detours. There are also sidetracks and dead ends. If you have been off the road for a while, it's time to get back on again. It's time to leave your past behind and go on to the beautiful and glorious future God has for you.

# NOTES

CHAPTER 4

1. L. J. West, et al., "Alcohol Consumption in the United States," *Annals of Internal Medicine* (1984), 405–416.

2. National Clearinghouse for Alcohol Information, 1981 *Fact Sheet*. Cf. also, A. Spickard and B. R. Thompson, *Dying for a Drink* (Waco, TX: Word, 1985).

3. R. M. Bennett, et al., "Alcohol and Human Physical Aggression," *Quarterly Journal Studies on Alcohol* (1969), 30.

4. *1984 Statistical Analysis,* (Washington, D.C.: United States Department of Commerce, 1984).

5. Cf. *Observer News,* 5–8, and D. W. Goodwin, "Alcohol in Suicide and Homicide," *Quarterly Journal Studies on Alcohol* (1973), 144.

6. See N. H. Woodward, *If Your Child is Drinking* (New York: Putnam, 1981), 10.

7. Ibid, 10–12.

8. Ibid, 12.

9. S. L. Englebardt, *Kids and Alcohol: The Deadliest Drug* (New York: Lothrop, Lee & Shepher, 1975), 9–15.

10. See the personal testimonies of Mark Only, *High* (Englewood Cliffs, NJ: Prentice-Hall, 1974) and Alexander De Jong, *Help and Hope for the Alcoholic* (Wheaton: Tyndale House, 1982). The latter is the personal account of a pastor who overcame alcoholism. See also Jay Strack, *Drugs and Drinking: What Every Teen and Parent Should Know* (Nashville: Thomas Nelson, 1985).

11. Robert Anastas, *The Contract for Life* (New York: Pocket Books/Simon and Schuster, 1985), 15. In this volume Anastas tells the story of the

formation of SADD in 1981 and the 33 percent drop since then in teenage deaths because of drunk driving.

12. R. A. Zucker, "Parental Influences on the Drinking Patterns of Their Children," in M. Greenblatt and M. Schuckit, eds., *Alcoholism Problems in Women and Children* (New York: Grune & Stratton, 1976).

13. Woodward, *If Your Child,* 21.

14. Ibid., 23–28.

15. Marian Sandmaier, *The Invisible Alcoholics* (New York: McGraw-Hill, 1980), 163–178, and John and Delores Langone, *Women Who Drink* (Reading, MA: Addison-Wesley, 1980), 109–122.

16. Robert McCormick, *Facing Alcoholism* (San Diego: Oak Tree Publications, 1982), 1–20.

17. J. R. DeFoe, W. Breed and L. A. Breed, "Drinking on Television: A Five-Year Study," *Journal of Drug Education* (1983), 25–38.

18. *1984 Statistical Analysis* (Washington, D.C.: United States Department of Commerce, 1984).

19. Linda Hindson, ed. *Facts About Mental Health and Chemical Addiction* (Lynchburg, VA: Virginia Baptist Hospital, 1987).

20. Cf. Englebardt, *Kids,* 46–48; T. R. Drews, *Getting Them Sober* (Plainfield, NJ: Bridge Publishing, 1983); Allan Luks, *Will America Sober Up?* (Boston: Beacon Press, 1983).

CHAPTER 5

1. Jay Strack, *Drugs and Drinking: What Every Teen and Parent Should Know* (Nashville: Thomas Nelson, rev. ed., 1985), 15. Consult this work for extensive treatment on dealing with alcohol and drugs. Copies can be obtained from your local bookstore, the publisher, or Jay Strack Ministries, P.O. Box 795377, Dallas, TX 75379; cf. also Freddie Gage, *Everything You Always Wanted To Know About Dope* (Houston: Pulpit Publications, 1971).

2. See David Augsburger, *So What? Everybody's Doing It!* (Chicago: Moody Press, 1969), 18, 19; and John Finlator, *The Drugged Nation* (New York: Simon & Schuster, 1973), 153–163.

3. See the comments of D. J. Baker, *A Generation at War with Itself* (New York: Viking Press, 1982); on the issue of adolescent rebellion, see Truman Dollar and Grace Ketterman, *Teenage Rebellion* (Old Tappan, NJ: Revell, 1980).

4. "Twelve Things You Should Know About Marijuana," *Consumer's Research* (April 1980), 1–10.

5. *High Times* (August, 1984).

6. "Teenage Drug Addiction," *USA Today* (October 3, 1984), C–1.

7. "Twelve Things You Should Know About Marijuana," *Consumer's Research* (April 1980), 8.

8. Gabriel G. Nahas, *Cocaine, The Great Addictor* (New York: Columbia University College of Physicians and Surgeons, 1982).

9. These points are developed from Dennis Nelson, *Adolescent Chemical Use Chart* (Minneapolis: Comp Care Publications, 1984). Used by permission.


CHAPTER 6

1. Charles Mylander, *Running the Red Lights: Putting the Brakes on Sexual Temptation* (Ventura, CA: Regal Books, 1986), 15. This is an extremely honest and helpful book every person battling sexual temptation ought to read.

2. Ibid.

3. Ella Wheeler Wilcox, "An Unfaithful Wife to Her Husband," *A Collection of Poems* (Boulder, CO: Blue Mountain Arts, 1975), 63.

4. J. Allen Peterson, *The Myth of the Greener Grass* (Wheaton: Tyndale House, 1983), 40.

5. See the insightful comments of Walter Byrd and Ed Hindson, *When the Road Gets Rough* (Old Tappan, NJ: Revell, 1986), 144–150.

6. Mylander, *Running,* 35.

7. Ibid., 36–38.

8. Ibid., 38.

9. For a technical discussion of deviant sexual behavior from a Christian standpoint, see William Backus, *Telling the Truth to Troubled People* (Minneapolis: Bethany House, 1985), 236–253.

10. Cf. Exodus 20:14; Matthew 5:28, 15:19; Leviticus 20:10–21; Proverbs 5:1–23, 7:21–22; 1 Corinthians 5:1–13; Romans 1:18–32, 13:14; Galatians 5:16–17; Jude 19.

11. According to Matthew 12:31–32 and Mark 3:28–29, the "unpardonable sin" is blasphemy against the Holy Spirit.

12. Cf. Gene Antonio, *The AIDS Cover Up?* (San Francisco: Ignatius Press, 1986); David Black, *The Plague Years: A Chronicle of AIDS* (New York: Simon & Schuster, 1985); Victor Gong and N. Rudnick, eds. *AIDS: Facts and Issues* (New Brunswick, NJ: Rutgers University Press, 1986); Randy Shilts, *And the Band Played On* (New York: St. Martin's Press, 1987).

13. Tim Timmons and Stephen Arterburn, *Hooked on Life* (Nashville: Oliver-Nelson, 1985), 125–126.

14. George Alan Reckers, *The Christian in the Age of Sexual Eclipse* (Wheaton: Tyndale House, 1981), 31.

15. David A. Seamands, *Healing for Damaged Emotions* (Wheaton: Victor Books, 1981), 22.

16. W. L. Coleman, *Bouncing Back* (Eugene, OR: Harvest House,

1985), 92. Cf. also this same theme throughout Dean Merrill, *Another Chance: How God Overrides Our Big Mistakes* (Grand Rapids: Zondervan, 1981).

17. Lewis Smedes, *Forgive and Forget* (San Francisco: Harper & Row, 1984), 73.

18. Mylander, *Running,* 206.

## CHAPTER 7

1. See the comments of Morton and Bernice Hunt, *The Divorce Experience* (New York: McGraw-Hill, 1987).

2. Cf. M. A. Fine, J. R. Moreland and A. I. Schwebel, "Long-term Effects of Divorce on Parent-Child Relationships," *Developmental Psychology,* vol. 19 (5), 1983, 703–710.

3. See his excellent work on divorce and remarriage. Edward G. Dobson, *What the Bible Really Says About Marriage, Divorce and Remarriage* (Old Tappan, NJ: Revell, 1986), 106.

4. Ibid.

5. See "Mental Health Interventions in Divorce Proceedings," *American Journal of Orthopsychiatry,* 48 (2), April 1978; and J. Wallerstein and J. Kelly, "Children and Divorce: A Review," *Social Work,* November 1979, 468–475.

6. Dobson, *What the Bible Really Says,* 107–109.

7. Wallerstein and Kelly, "Children and Divorce," 264.

8. Judson J. Swihart and Steven L. Brigham, *Helping Children of Divorce* (Downers Grove, IL: InterVarsity Press, 1982), 39. Used by permission.

9. Dobson, *What the Bible Really Says,* 110–111.

10. Ed Hindson, *The Total Family* (Wheaton: Tyndale House, 1980). 114–115.

11. Morton and Bernice Hunt, *Divorce,* 5. They note that over 500 books and articles have been written about divorce in the last ten years.

12. John Splinter, *Second Chapter: New Beginnings After Separation or Divorce* (Grand Rapids: Baker, 1987), 33–45.

13. Ibid., 140. Splinter discusses this at length. His advice is practical, biblical, and sound.

14. Lonnie Barbach, "Sexuality," in A. Villoldo and K. Dychtwald, eds., *Millennium: Glimpses in the 21st Century* (Los Angeles: J. P. Tarcher, 1981), 35.

15. Ibid., 36.

16. See Splinter, *Second Chapter,* 171–203.

CHAPTER 8

1. See the striking study by M. A. Strauss, R. J. Gelles and S. K. Steinmetz, *Behind Closed Doors: Violence in the American Family* (Garden City, NY: Doubleday, 1980). Statistics quoted throughout the text.

2. Samuel X. Radbill, "A History of Child Abuse and Infanticide," in *The Battered Child.*, R. E. Helfer and C. H. Kempe, eds. (Chicago: University of Chicago Press, 1974).

3. See David Gil, *Violence Against Children: Physical Child Abuse in the United States* (Cambridge, MA: Harvard University Press, 1981), 71–90.

4. Boston *Globe* (February 6, 1973), 12.

5. J. Bourouris, "Homicide and the Family," in *Journal of Marriage and the Family* (November, 1971), 667–677.

6. R. I. Parnas, "The Police Response to Domestic Disturbance," *Wisconsin Law Review,* (Fall 1967), 914–960.

7. See Strauss, Gelles and Steinmetz, *Behind Closed Doors,* 60–63 for detailed statistics.

8. *The Real Paper* (February 5, 1975), 18, quoted by Strauss, Gelles, and Steinmetz, 66.

9. D. Bakan, *Slaughter of the Innocents: A Study of the Battered Child Phenomenon* (Boston: Beacon Press, 1971).

10. A. Button, "Some Antecedents of Felonious and Delinquent Behavior," *Journal of Clinical Child Psychology* (Fall, 1973), 35–38.

11. R. S. Welsh, "Severe Parental Punishment and Delinquency: A Development Theory," *Journal of Clinical Child Psychology* (Winter 1976), 17–21.

12. Strauss, Gelles and Steinmetz, *Behind Closed Doors,* 211.

13. David Gil, *Violence,* 140–141. This study also revealed that the highest incidence of reported child abuse occur in California, Texas, New York, Pennsylvania and Michigan. The highest percentage of reported child abuse in relation to the total population occurred in Texas, Maryland, California, Nevada and Michigan.

14. Quoted by G. B. Blaine, *Are Parents Bad for Children?* (New York: Coward, McCann & Geoghegan, 1973), 90.

15. For a detailed discussion of appropriate child discipline, see James Dobson, *Dare to Discipline* (Wheaton: Tyndale House, 1970), 21 ff.

16. Dobson, *Dare,* 25–50. Cf. also *Dr. Dobson Answers Your Questions About Raising Children* (Wheaton: Tyndale House, 1982).

17. James Dobson, *Hide or Seek* (Old Tappan, NJ: Revell, 1979), 61. In this book Dobson develops several key factors which contribute to a healthy self-image, as well as pointing out barriers to its development.

18. See Blaine, *Are Parents Bad,* 71.

## CHAPTER 9

1. For a detailed psychological explanation of the effect of incest on both fathers and daughters, see Jean Renvoize, *Incest: A Family Pattern* (London: Routledge & Kegan Paul, 1982), 7–23.

2. A. Rosenfeld, "The Clinical Management of Incest and Sexual Abuse of Children," *Journal of the American Medical Association* (Oct. 19, 1979), 1761–64; and "Incidence of a History of Incest Among Eighteen Female Psychiatric Patients," *American Journal of Psychiatry* (1979), 791–795.

3. Report of the Harborview Medical Center in Seattle, Washington, on 593 children under the age of sixteen who were sexually molested between October 1977 and August 1979. Quoted by Renvoize, op.cit., 27.

4. See Blair and Rita Justice, *The Broken Taboo: Sex in the Family* (New York: Human Sciences Press, 1979), 15–34.

5. M. Tsai and N. Wagner, "Incest and Molestation: Problems of Childhood Sexuality," *Resident and Staff Physician* (March, 1979), 129–136. They note, however, that boys are less likely to report sexual advances by older women because they tend not to view themselves as victims in such encounters.

6. See Renvoize, *Incest*, 30. This same view is expressed by D. Finkelhor, "Sex Among Siblings," *Archives of Sexual Behavior*, (1980), 171–194.

7. Blair and Justice, *The Broken Taboo*, 63 ff.

8. Ibid., 64.

9. Ibid.

10. Ibid., 165–166.

## CHAPTER 10

1. For an excellent popular study of rape, its psychological effects, and the potential for recovery, see Helen Benedict, *Recovery: How to Survive Sexual Assault* (Garden City, NY: Doubleday, 1985).

2. Ibid., 19.

3. Ibid.

4. See the insightful study of Ann Burgess and Lynda Holmstrom, *Rape: Crisis and Recovery* (Bowie, MD: Brady, 1979).

5. Benedict, *Recovery*, 1.

6. Ellen Frank, *The Rape Victim: Her Response and Treatment* (Pittsburgh: Western Psychiatric Institute, 1979).

7. A. N. Groth and H. J. Birnbaum, *Men Who Rape: The Psychology of the Offender* (New York: Plenum Press, 1979).

8. Benedict, *Recovery*, 10.

9. Ibid., 43.

10. Susan Brownmiller, *Against Our Will: Men, Women and Rape*

(New York: Simon & Schuster, 1975), 270 ff.; and Rochel Grossman, ed., *Surviving Sexual Assault* (New York: Congdon & Weed, 1983), 18 ff.

11. "A Letter from a Victim," in *Emotional First-Aid for Teens* (New York: St. Vincent's Rape Crisis Center, n.d.), quoted in Benedict, *Recovery,* 196.


CHAPTER 11

1. Cf. P. Cameron, "Abortion," in D. G. Benner, ed., *Baker Encyclopedia of Psychology* (Grand Rapids: Baker, 1985), 8–9; and "Legal Abortion Seen in 30 Per Cent of Pregnancies," in *Washington Post* (January 9, 1980).

2. Cameron, "Abortion," 8–9.

3. James Hitchcock, *What is Secular Humanism?* (Ann Arbor, MI: Servant Books, 1982), 102–104.

4. Jerry Falwell, *If I Should Die Before I Wake* (Nashville: Thomas Nelson, 1986). Every person concerned with the issue of abortion and the provision of a creative alternative needs to read this powerful book.

5. Ibid., 146.

6. See the comments of Francis A. Schaeffer and C. Everett Koop, *Whatever Happened to the Human Race?* (Old Tappan, NJ: Revell, 1979). This entire volume is also included in *The Complete Works of Francis A. Schaeffer* (Westchester, IL: Crossway Books, 1982), vol. 5, 280–410.

7. John T. Noonan, "Why a Constitutional Amendment?" *Human Life Review* (1975), 28.

8. Archibald Cox, *The Role of the Supreme Court in American Government* (New York: Oxford University Press, 1976).

9. Schaeffer and Koop, *Whatever Happened,* 294.

10. See Jerry Falwell, *Listen America!* (Garden City, NY: Doubleday, 1980), 165–180.


CHAPTER 12

1. Dean Merrill, *Another Chance: How God Overrides Our Big Mistakes* (Grand Rapids: Zondervan, 1981), 15.

2. Erwin Lutzer, *Failure: The Back Door to Success* (Chicago: Moody Press, 1975), 83.

3. Ed Hindson and Walt Byrd, *When the Road Gets Rough* (Old Tappan, NJ: Revell, 1986), 77.

4. Charles Swindoll, *Starting Over* (Portland, OR: Multnomah Press, 1977), 9.

# BIBLIOGRAPHY

Anastas, Robert. *The Contract for Life*. New York: Pocket Books, 1985.

Augsburger, David. *So What? Everybody's Doing It!* Chicago: Moody Press, 1969.

Bakan, D. *Slaughter of the Innocents: A Study of the Battered Child Phenomenon*. Boston: Beacon Press, 1971.

Baker, D. J. *A Generation at War with Itself*. New York: Viking Press, 1982.

Benedict, Helen. *Recovery: How to Survive Sexual Assault*. Garden City, NY: Doubleday, 1985.

Brenton, Myron. *The Runaways*. Boston: Little, Brown & Co., 1978.

Brownmiller, Susan. *Against Our Will: Men, Women and Rape*. New York: Simon & Schuster, 1975.

Burgess, Ann and Lynda Holstrom. *Rape: Crisis and Recovery*. Bowie, MD: Brady, 1979.

Carroll, Anne K. *From the Brink of Divorce*. Garden City, NY: Doubleday, 1978.

Coleman, W. L. *Bouncing Back*. Eugene, OR: Harvest House, 1985.

Decter, Midge. *Liberal Parents, Radical Children*. New York: Coward, McCann, & Geoghegan, 1975.

De Jong, Alexander. *Help and Hope for the Alcoholic*. Wheaton: Tyndale House, 1982.

Dobson, Edward G. *What the Bible Really Says About Marriage, Divorce and Remarriage*. Old Tappan, NJ: Revell, 1986.

Dobson, James. *Dare to Discipline*. Wheaton: Tyndale House, 1970.

  *Dr. Dobson Answers Your Questions About Raising Children*. Wheaton: Tyndale House, 1986.

Dollar, Truman and Grace Ketterman. *Teenage Rebellion*. Old Tappan, NJ: Revell, 1980.

Englebardt, S. L. *Kids and Alcohol: The Deadliest Drug*. New York: Lothrop, Lee & Shepher, 1975.

Epstein, Joseph. *Divorced in America*. New York: E. P. Dutton & Co. 1974.

Falwell, Jerry. *If I Should Die Before I Wake*. Nashville: Thomas Nelson, 1986.

Finlator, John. *The Drugged Nation*. New York: Simon & Schuster, 1973.

Fontana, V. J. *Somewhere a Child is Crying*. New York: Macmillan, 1973.

Frank, Ellen. *The Rape Victim*. Pittsburgh: Western Psychiatric Institute, 1979.

Gil, David G. *Violence Against Children*. Cambridge, MA: Harvard University Press, 1973.

Grossman, Rachel. *Surviving Sexual Assault*. New York: Congdon & Weed, 1983.

Hindson, Ed. *The Total Family*. Wheaton: Tyndale House, 1980.

Hindson, Ed and Walt Byrd. *When the Road Gets Rough*. Old Tappan, NJ: Revell, 1986.

Hitchcock, James. *What is Secular Humanism?* Ann Arbor, MI: Servant Books, 1982.

Hunt, Morton and Bernice. *The Divorce Experience*. New York: McGraw-Hill, 1977.

Janus, Sam. *The Death of Innocence: How Children are Endangered by the New Sexual Freedom*. New York: Morrow, 1981.

Justice, Blair and Rita. *The Broken Taboo: Sex in the Family*. New York: Human Sciences Press, 1978.

Keniston, Kenneth. *All Our Children: The American Family Under Pressure*. New York: Harcourt, Brace & Jovanovich, 1977.

Levine, David. *How to Get a Divorce*. New York: Bantam Books, 1979.

Luks, Allen. *Will America Sober Up?* Boston: Beacon Press, 1983.

Martin, Del. *Battered Wives*. San Francisco: Glide Publications, 1976.

Merrill, Dean. *Another Chance: How God Overrides Our Big Mistakes*. Grand Rapids: Zondervan, 1981.

Mylander, Charles. *Running the Red Lights: Putting the Brakes on Sexual Temptation*. Ventura, CA: Regal Books, 1986.

Nahas, Gabriel G. *Cocaine: The Great Addictor*. New York: Columbia University Press, 1982.

O'Neill, G. K. *2081: A Hopeful View of the Human Future*. New York: Simon & Schuster, 1981.

Only, Mark. *High*. Englewood Cliffs, NJ: Prentice-Hall, 1974.

Peterson, J. Allen. *The Myth of the Greener Grass*. Wheaton: Tyndale House, 1983.

Radbill, S. X. *The Battered Child*. Chicago: University of Chicago Press, 1974.

Reckers, G. A. *The Christian in the Age of Sexual Eclipse*. Wheaton: Tyndale House, 1981.

Renvoize, Jean. *Incest: A Family Pattern*. London: Routledge & Kegan Paul, 1982.

Sandmaier, Marian. *The Invisible Alcoholics*. New York: McGraw-Hill, 1980.

Schaeffer, Francis A. and C. Everett Koop, *Whatever Happened to the Human Race?* Old Tappan, NJ: Revell, 1979.

Schechter, Susan. *Women and Male Violence*. Boston: South End Press, 1982.

Seamands, David A. *Healing for Damaged Emotions*. Wheaton: Victor Books, 1981.

Shorter, Edward. *The Making of the Modern Family*. New York: Basic Books, 1975.

Smedes, Lewis. *Forgive and Forget*. San Francisco: Harper & Row, 1984.

Splinter, John. *Second Chapter: New Beginnings after Separation and Divorce*. Grand Rapids: Baker, 1987.

Stanley, Charles. *How to Keep Your Kids on Your Team*. Nashville: Thomas Nelson, 1986.

Strack, Jay. *Drugs and Drinking: What Every Teen and Parent Should Know*. Nashville: Thomas Nelson, 1985.

Strauss, M. A., R. J. Gelles, and S. K. Stienmetz. *Behind Closed Doors: Violence in the American Family*. Garden City, NY: Doubleday, 1980.

Swindoll, Charles R. *Starting Over: Fresh Hope for the Road Ahead*. Portland, OR: Multnomah Press, 1977.

Timmons, Tim and Stephen Arterburn, *Hooked On Life*. Nashville: Oliver-Nelson, 1985.

Villoldo, A. and K. Dychtwald, eds. *Millennium: Glimpses Into the 21st Century*. Los Angeles: Tarcher, 1981.

Walker, Lenore. *The Battered Woman*. New York: Harper & Row, 1979.

Weitzman, L. J. *The Divorce Revolution*. New York: Macmillan, 1985.

Woodward, N. H. *If Your Child Is Drinking*. New York: G. Putnam's Sons, 1981.

*Jay Strack is in the ministry to help hurting people.
If you have been challenged or convicted by reading
this book and want further help, write to him today.
If you, too, have a victory testimony to share of how
you have been helped by this book, please send it to
him. If you would like to volunteer to help others
by sharing your testimony, please let us know. You
can write to:*

JAY STRACK
JAY STRACK ASSOCIATION
P.O. BOX 795337
DALLAS, TX 75379